More Fiya

More Fiya

a New Collection of Black British Poetry

edited by

Kayo Chingonyi

CANONGATE

First published in Great Britain, the USA and Canada in 2022
by Canongate Books Ltd, 14 High Street, Edinburgh EH1 1TE

Distributed in the USA by Publishers Group West and in Canada
by Publishers Group Canada

canongate.co.uk

1

British Library Cataloguing-in-Publication Data
A catalogue record for this book is available on
request from the British Library

ISBN 978 1 83885 530 7

Typeset in Bembo by
Palimpsest Book Production Ltd, Falkirk, Stirlingshire

Printed and bound in Great Britain by Clays Ltd, Elcograf S.p.A.

For those who come after,
in love and fellowship

Contents

Kayo Chingonyi
Introduction 1

Jason Allen-Paisant
Maple Grove 9
Learning Birdsong 10
Tree Dreaming 11

Raymond Antrobus
The Acceptance 12
And That 14
For Cousin John 16

Dean Atta
No Ascension 18
Signet 20
Two Black Boys in Paradise 22

Janette Ayachi
The Lovers 24
QuickFire, Slow Burning 26
Worshipping Grief 29

Dzifa Benson
For the Love of Hendrik de Jongh, Drummer from Batavia 31
Ms Hipson, the tall Dutchwoman, dreams of dancing with a man tall enough to make her feel delicate 34
Ms Sidonia married twice and retired a wealthy woman 35

Malika Booker
Points of this Reckoning 36
Discordant Mourning 40
Golden Grove 41

Eric Ngalle Charles
Mboa Mi: 'My Country' 44
Heroes 45
A Song for Freedom 48

Inua Ellams
The Vanishing 49
Of Howling Wolves 51
A Boy / Twice 52

Samatar Elmi
[Etymologies] 54
The Fear 56
Coda 58

Khadijah Ibrahiim
Herman Avenue
Hand-Cart Woman 60
Bath Prescription 1 65
Bush Craft Prescription 68

Keith Jarrett
My mother sings of how she got her education 70
Scalp 71
Nor the Arrow That Flies in the Day 73

Anthony Joseph
Naming 75
Wire, God of Wallerfield 78
House Party, Mt Lambert, 1978 79

Safiya Kamaria Kinshasa
Bitch Ghazal 80
Hurricanes Also Taught Us How to Be Sophisticated When Things Get Messy 82
Slow Whine 83

Vanessa Kisuule
Auntiehood 85
Blessings 86
On Freezing A Dead Son 88

Rachel Long
Your Daddy Ain't Rich 90
As If 92

Adam Lowe
Desire 93
Aftermath 95
Once We Were Wolves 97

Nick Makoha
An Essay on Man 98
Pythagoras Theorem 100
The Long Duration of a Split Second 102

Karen McCarthy Woolf
from Unsafe 104

Momtaza Mehri
A Comparative History of Fire 108
hooyos 110
Even on Canvas, Oilfields Burn 111

Bridget Minamore
Golden Shovel for My People 113
Catching Joke 115
Sestina for Kara Walker 118

Selina Nwulu
A History of Banning 120
Mango Tree 121
When the Party Is Over 123

Gboyega Odubanjo
Dip 124
Arrangements 125
Man 126

Louisa Adjoa Parker
There are moments I forget 127
You're 129
Housewarming 130

Roger Robinson
Gold 131
Aba Shanti Soundsystem 132

Denise Saul
The Room Between Us 133
Instructions For Yellow 134
The Viewing 135

Kim Squirrell
Walking Home from School 136
Healing 137
I Want to Write a Poem About Togetherness 138

Warsan Shire
Backwards 140
Midnight in the Foreign Food Aisle 142

Rommi Smith
from Palette for a Portrait of Little Richard 143

Yomi Ṣode
On Fatherhood: Proximity to Death 146
[Insert Name]'s Mother: A Ghazal 149
On Fatherhood: Envy 151

Degna Stone
over 152
Another Tongue 154
How to Unpick the Lies? 155

Keisha Thompson
Some Have Beaten Suffering 157
The Concrete Square off Tib Street in May 159
Number 2020 160

Kandace Siobhan Walker
Art Pop 164
Eye Contact 165
Sugar, Sugar, Honey, Honey 166

Warda Yassin
Swift 167
Treetop Hotel 168
Miss Yassin 169

Belinda Zhawi
Tchaikovsky's January 170
Runyengetero 172
This Body Wants What It Wants 173

Contributors 175
Acknowledgements 189
Permission Acknowledgements 191

Introduction

WHEN I WAS SEVENTEEN, I joined a workshop group run by the writer development agency Spread the Word and the live literature production company Apples and Snakes. The purpose of these fortnightly workshops was to foment poetic practice and encourage kinship between writers. There was the sense of an open syllabus inclusive not just of the practices of versification but also the matter of being in the world and flourishing in a context unfit for black people to flourish (as human beings let alone literary artists). Community (one's commitment to and indivisibility from it) was the guiding ethos.

This sat in stark contrast to the machinations of the literary establishment at that time which I can best illustrate with an anecdote. At this early stage of my public writing life, I met the editor of a venerated poetry journal who made it clear, without having seen anything I'd written, that mine was not the kind of work they published in the pages of their magazine. I didn't send poems to that magazine until a guest editor, a Black British guest editor, invited me to do so more than ten years later. There were clear divisions in the poetry ecosystem across boundaries of race, class, and most definitely gender. The brightest stars in that literary firmament were a crop of mostly straight, mostly white, men writing in a mainstream post-war lyric tradition which foregrounded a certain kind of poetic excellence over and above others. To flourish in this world, so the received wisdom ran, meant adopting, and adapting to, a poetic voice which might best be classified by the word 'craft'; the operative word in a recent essay by Rebecca Watts which indulges essentialist terms for measuring literary excellence. The arguments put forth in the piece, which I won't rehash here at length, rang with an implicit call to *simpler times* in which 'poetry was an artform'.* Part of this ossified idea of poetic craft – *work showing the expenditure of skill and expertise* – hinges on a stable image of the poet as *professional*; another word freighted with unspoken value. The problem with this is that it is a model of writing practice based on exclusivity, reinscribing ideas of scarcity. If we read poetry in this light, then there are finite resources of excellence open only to those poets who work hardest. But on whose terms is this hard work quantified?

The community into which I was allowed to step as a beginning poet existed mostly in the live performance arena, rather than in print publication. So, my early practice as a poet involved getting together enough poems to form a set that I might perform live at an open mic night with a view to being booked to perform a longer set at an established

* Rebecca Watts, 'The Cult of the Noble Amateur', in *PN Review* 239, Volume 44 Number 3, January–February 2018

event series. The publication, the making public, I was working towards was a site-specific form of publication, a communal form. This is an origin story so ubiquitous among Black British Poets as to seem contrived. And it was. If you overwhelmingly consign Black British Poets to the live arena, as indeed was the norm between the 70s and late 90s in the UK, then it becomes possible to say that there is an *essential* difference between these poets and those who seemed to occupy the prime real estate in poetry, the avenues of prestige. Indeed, this is exactly what the mostly white, mostly male editorati said to defend themselves from charges of institutional unconscious bias against Black British Poets. These poets were simply not good enough to be publishable, or their writing worked best in the live context, there was no audience for this kind of poetry. In short, the message was the same as that which I received from *the venerated editor* at seventeen: *though we will not look at them, your poems do not interest us*. The fault was always said to be the poets'. We black poets have, for a long time, known otherwise. Anyone who hasn't been licking the underside of a rock buried in the sand will grasp the importance of Black British aesthetics to the continued life and dynamism of British Poetry as a whole. For my part, though I'm known for my published work, relationships fostered on the live scene are the foundational interrogative and aesthetic relations my work inhabits to this day, and if they have enlivened my poetics, I wonder what they have done for the countless poets who share a trajectory like mine.

For such poets, visibility in the world of publication was the stuff of speculative fiction. Before we had the abundance of poetry collections by Black British Poets that seems now, at long last, to be in the offing, the poetry anthology was our principal space of possibility as published poets. I am thinking here of such anthologies as *Bittersweet*, *Kin*, *IC3*, *A Storm Between Fingers*, and, of course, *The Fire People*. I first read *The Fire People* when I was nineteen or twenty. The poems that were being held up as exemplary (in the syllabus of my university degree and in the pages of poetry magazines) did not speak, or look, like me. Here at last was a poetics of skin; of the barbershop; nightclub; the corner; the family dinner table; church; the foci of my life outside white institutions. These were poems in which my life had value because it could stand in for the lives of others. Such anthologies saved me, in several senses of the word, beginning a restlessness and indignation that is the essential thread of my work as a writer, editor, and scholar alike.

We live in a cultural landscape that regards visibility alone as a sign of change. If more black poets are getting published, receiving institutional largesse, editing, performing and otherwise taking up space, this must mean the work is almost done. I contend that the work these landmark volumes set out is merely in its infancy. The radicalism in these volumes was to show black life as normal rather than as a deviation from the norm of whiteness. These anthologies, in other words, complicate the idea of a stable audience for poetry by extending the poetic notion of what it's like to be in the world and, as well, what it is like to be in the world in a black skin. While our poetry has been denigrated as revelling in identity politics, we know this critique for the dog-whistle it is. Our lives can stand in for the lives of others because our lives are equally valuable. I'm reminded, here, of Michael Che's stand-up show *Matters* which, among other things, serves as an extended close reading of the impact of the phrase 'Black Lives Matter' on the edifices of structural whiteness. How dare we say that? And yet, in our poems, in the careful weaving of our cultural praxis, we have been saying it in defiant, quiet, soulful, pained, and opaque ways for decades. It's just that lately swathes of people outside our circle seem to be listening. The abundance we now witness, evidenced by the clarity, scope and ambition of the poems collected in these pages (and the many more that you won't find here but must seek out) are not the product of some overnight sensation. They are the product of community, ingenuity and persistence in the face of overwhelming pressures to the contrary.

Speaking of having to seek things out, my approach in assembling this anthology owes much to my background as a record collector and DJ. The sound artist Ain Bailey expressed the artistry of the DJ particularly well in thinking about the form of the record box; a finite space into which a DJ must place those records that might best mash up the dance, rebuild it, and mash it up again. The box can only hold so many records and, so, preparing for a DJ set is a matter not just of playing what is known but finding new kinships and resonances between tracks someone hasn't thought to play together. In the end, when you turn up to the venue and stand in front of the decks you respond in the moment, you find the right tune for an always evolving present. The limitations of the form dictate that you can't have your entire collection with you, there will be gaps for the dancers to fill with implication; finding, in the unfamiliar, the ripples of a groove they know.

As it is with the DJ, so it is with the anthologist. One person could never hope to cover the breadth of Black British Poetry. I have not tried to do so. Instead, I present here a selection of poems which vibrate across a spectrum of Black British aesthetics broadly conceived. In these pages you'll find chimerical re-makings of the Caribbean, the wisdom of diasporic philosophy, the cold and rain of Blighty, the sky viewed from the African continent, and the rhythms of language shifting before your eyes and in your ears. These are poems connected by the thread of variety; narrative jostling with sonic and spatially engaged units of poetic sense to break open language's capacity to mean and re-sound. These are, to borrow the words of Paul Gilroy, 'Black Atlantic' poems. It strikes me that Gilroy's words might constitute a durable set of organising principles for Black British Poetry. According to Gilroy the Black Atlantic is a name for:

> The stereophonic, bilingual, or bifocal cultural forms originated by, but no longer the exclusive property of, blacks dispersed within the structures of feeling, producing, communicating and remembering.*

I want here, briefly, to celebrate the work of those who came before. While this can only ever be a partial genealogy, let the gaps be filled in your mind as you read this, and as you embark on your own quest to plant afresh the cuttings from the vast and assiduously tended garden that is Black British Poetry. Hail up: the Afro Style School, Urban Poets

---

* Paul Gilroy, *The Black Atlantic: Modernity and Double Consciousness* (London: Verso, 1993)

Society, Malika's Poetry Kitchen, Mannafest, Apricot Jam, Commonword, flipped eye, the George Padmore Institute, Bogle-L'Ouverture, Payback Press, The Complete Works, Obsidian Foundation and all those flashpoints of communality connecting Black British Poets to their poetic heritage in the absence of a proper chronicle.

Kayo Chingonyi, 2021

Jason Allen-Paisant

Maple Grove

I proceed
      light sieved

trying to identify
      birdsong

in maple leaves   I am escaping
      chores

my church of work
      is always

a cool evergreen
      always   where

the landscape transforms
      to a new body

Learning Birdsong

verbs clear the head
& enter the flesh
birds are nearer
nouns the spirits
of occasions
I catch a song &
five others escape
a noun cannot hold
the sound of birds
the woodland always
is poem
awaiting
do not forget
this

Tree Dreaming

Last night I dreamt
a tree was dreaming
me
all night
I was trying
to decipher
I can't carry
its knowledge
into the waking
with me   instead
I reach always
over into the dream-t

but it did speak
to me it did   right there
I heard the language &
confirmed what I had known
I told this tree to keep on
coming   I'd grow
more receptive
to its language
so that I might
carry it out of
this vision
with me

Raymond Antrobus

The Acceptance

Dad's house stands again, four years
after being demolished. I walk in.
He lies in bed, licks his rolling paper,
and when I ask *Where have you been?*
We buried you. He says *I know,*

I know. I lean into his smoke, tell him
I went back to Jamaica, I met your brothers,
losing you made me need them. He says
something I don't hear. *What?* Moving lips,
no sound. I shake my head. He frowns.

Disappears. I wake in the hotel room,
heart drumming. I get up slowly, the floor
is wet. I wade into the bathroom,
my father standing by the sink, all the taps
running. He laughs and takes

my hand, squeezes, his ring
digs into my flesh. I open my eyes again.
I'm by a river, a shimmering sheet
of green marble. Red ants crawl up
an oak tree's flaking bark. My hands

are cold mud. I follow the tall grass
by the riverbank, the song, my deaf Orisha
of music, Oshun, in brass bracelets and earrings,
bathes my father in a white dress. I wave, *Hey!*

She keeps singing. The dress turns the river
gold and there's my father surfacing.
He holds a white and green drum. I watch him
climb out the water, drip towards Oshun.
They embrace. My father beats his drum.
With shining hands, she signs: *Welcome.*

And That

(after seeing a childhood friend outside a chicken shop in Dalston)

Chicken wings / and dat
Boss man / salt in them / and dat

Don't assault man / give man a nap-
Kin / big man / no steroid / and dat

Dark times / new street lights / and dat
How's man? / I'm getting by / and dat

Still / boy dem / harass
Not beefin' / not tagged / man / still trapped

Cycle man / peddlin' / and dat
On road / new pavements / levelled / and dat

Crackney changed / still / stay dwelling / and dat
Paradise moves / but I got to land grab

We E8 / East man / ain't got to adapt
Our Kingdom / got no land to hand back

Man / chat breeze / chat
Trade winds / and dat

You out ends / got good job / legit / and dat?
Locked off man dem / stay plotting / and dat

Rah, Ray / flower shorts? / You hipster / in dat
Man gone / vegan? / No chicken wings / and dat

For Cousin John

land of shades!
William Blake

Your voice, a red and white flag,
a teatime tablecloth. *Slavery*

happened long ago, it means
nothing now. I prepare silence,

practise each time for a calm dinner

but you lift a fork, unsettle the territory.

I can't stop seeing the child
pulled from a home of hissing

and raised by our grandmother
who was endlessly scraping plates

between us. With her gone

something shifts at our table and you

keep sharpening the somewhere else
in me. No, I don't know what it's like

to live in a small military town
or how you fit where everyone is white.

Do you hold up England

by its gilt edges, best china handles?

What secretly stirs your tea? *Cousin,*
we all alone in these streets. I wish you

horses in rain and fields of broken gates.
I wish you a surprise party of sober mothers

holding Thomas the Tank Engine birthday cake.
I wish you glistening grapes and radiated rooms.

When we stood shoulder to shoulder
at our grandmother's funeral I didn't hear you cry

but I felt your quivering, saw your red face,
the fallen flags in your eyes, Cousin, why couldn't you

let us see what you were burying? Cousin

I wish sunlight on all your fields

Dean Atta

No Ascension

You are in hospital, so we buy plane tickets.
You are dying when we reach your bedside.
You are dead, so we wear black for forty days.
Forty days are over but I'm still wearing black.

In London no one knows why.
In Cyprus, we moved as one
black cloud of grief, the whole family
dressed in the same colour.

Either side of your grave I was black.
And this isn't a eulogy, it's about me.
How I haven't cleaned the mud from your grave
off the shoes I bought for your funeral.

How often I look at the photos I took of you
smiling, dying, dead, and being buried.
How your watch and prayer beads are in the
  drawer
of the desk I am writing this poem on.

How grief makes much more sense to me
than feeling depressed when times are good.

How a grandfather is meant to die old
and surrounded by his family, just as you did.

How my notebook is a grave and my laptop
is a grave, how my phone is a grave and my bed
is a grave, and there was no ascension after
forty days. And I have stayed buried, with you.

Signet

Your engraved ring reads D.M.P.
If I hadn't changed my surname
this would have been left to me

We are making each other pay
for an inherited debt
your brother my father

the push and pull between
us an elastic band
in the hands of a restless student

We have grown with this tension
yet never snapped
back at each other

and without fail
every time you would drive me home
you would call out 'I love you' as I exited the car

I wanted to crush and crumple you – screaming
'I would trade a million uncles for just one father –
drive your brother back and make him love me!'

Instead I said nothing
not 'I love you too'
not 'I love you too much'

not 'I wish you were my father
so I could have kept my surname'
I turned my key in the front door
I didn't turn back

I heard your engine humming
you hadn't gone
you were waiting

Two Black Boys in Paradise

They won't be here forever,
maybe just as long as this poem.
These two black boys in paradise.
Two black boys: can you see them?

These two black boys are free.
These two black boys are happy.
Black boys are real boys.
Black boys are not just little men.

Do you believe black boys
are real, like for real for real?
Real black boys feel.
These two black boys are a healing.

Did you poison the apple already?
Did you dig up the tree?
Are you trying to plant
these black boys in the ground?

Did you call them apple thieves?
Did you call the police?
There are no police in paradise.
There are no white people in this paradise.

The two boys in this poem have black boy names.
They have grown up now,
but their names still suit them.
Masculinity has not been required of them.

They are in love with each other,
and they are in love with themselves.
One kisses the other's Adam's apple.
They don't make babies.

Maybe paradise is just meant for two people at a time.
Maybe it will be two black girls in paradise next time.
Maybe they won't have to be
boys or girls.

Maybe it will be you in paradise
with that person
you have in mind
right now.

Janette Ayachi

The Lovers

He wakes and grunts incalculable words,
stirring like a sleeping giant in a cartoon forest.
I fall asleep with my arm slung over his chest,
it lifts up hard and high with each inhale
and latches down to the mattress with each exhale.
His lungs are heavy. Asthmatic. Bulky. Bullied as a child.
I am hugging a wounded reindeer
that has taken an arrow for me.
I feel where his antlers protrude
under the tendrils of his blond curls.
A dandy. A decade my junior.
Filmmaker; from Bauhaus to daytime television.
All his heroic strength stored in the swell
and steal from limp to pulse in the flex of my wrist.
Still, she comes eating olives
and holding her breath for flowers.
Both my lovers have short clavicles:
they are landscapes without tourists
eager for my sensualities.
'Dress me in drool' I imagine them together whispering.
I have an IPA afternoon, and end up
dancing with a sandwich.
Meat eaters; their carnage seeps through their pores,

loud music and no love, it happens, hard hats and
November rain.
After, I treat myself
to the most expensive whisky in an Art Deco hotel.
Is Jupiter open tonight? I ask the barman.
Quiet continues.
Life wipes itself clean,
and twigs outside hold the circumference of dusk.
What are those racehorses running to on the screen?
No sooner does one hoof meet the next
than it disperses into air.
Unlit fields on my eyelids, I feel something
more innocuous,
like watching the sun descend
into a body of water for hours,
island cosmology; some people
are too potent to take home.
It's not just a decision I make, it's the clock and its
throwback mentality;
look at how I can make you
disconnect from time's assertions
and now, see how I can make you remember them?
A constant tug of war between worlds –
nothing is hidden,
we are merely forgetting what it is
we are looking for –
after being so long engulfed against the mantle of dark.
So shoot for me again, offer me another chance tomorrow
and all tomorrows, send me a vision, another direction
towards Vesta, my hearth and home;
flame felt at the tail of my spine.

QuickFire, Slow Burning

Fire is malicious. It comes quickly but takes its delight in burning slowly. Love is like this. Grief. All that space now after the chasms of fire; burning Amazonian forests, Californian wildfires, Australian bushfires. The lungs of the earth coughing up a phlegm of choking parrots, charred coyotes, polluted sea.

In 1666, a year after the Great Plague began, four days of fire reaped through the slums of London, timber frames tumbled, bakeries on Pudding Lane melted, people threw their furniture into the Thames. The fiery vermillion pavements swallowed a squall of rats whole, wiping the vermin spread. London Bridge burnt down, and the inferno stripped the city to a smouldering ruin.

When Notre-Dame caught fire last year holy candles and burning plates broke the land, roof destroyed and spire collapsed; the external disk and dharma, the djinns, lightning striking the pyramids, safe blue skies topped with a dynamite red. We are making history smoky again at the time of a pandemic.

Smoke is both signal and toxin, the heat rules forwards and inwards like a dislocation of longing because language doesn't stand still, it waits for no one. All the coins have been taken from the well, gamblers diced a fist in the mouth, one shot of a carbon-kiss for a lucky charm and the flames bring in the wealth of rattling bones.

Life is our laboratory, a seatbelt for invention and rejuvenation as we crash test final frontiers of knowledge and all walks of life. We are not meant to be slaves and drones, but divine beings releasing old patterns by staring into the abyss that appears in the centre of itself, despite the danger, as it stares back at you. Like all things that cross arms in Parliament, angry phantoms appear; what happens behind the scenes?

Television reflects reality, reality reflects television; a gold locket on a necklace carrying two frayed dead parents by the heads. Hong Kong roars up with protest, tear-gas blowers, the subtleties unhinged, teenagers are missing, the last photograph, time spreads her wings.

Unable to take flight again until the unknown future, I place myself in this corner house of stone and moonrise, embossed by what is left behind, whitewash emulsion, planned and preordained to support the illusion it creates. It is the best place I've ever seen, still, I'm ready to explore more, as the internet feeds me images of unimaginable landscapes; cultures, kills, the love sicknesses coloured by what the crop can carry into two back gardens, all those new smells and bright sounds, life resuming as normal, an evolved normal, life tweaking its résumé after a gap year in Pandemonia instead of Cambodia.

This morning traces of fire cause an orange tint to the cirrus clouds, aerosols transported from North America, my heart resists melting in my chest and escapes the hot-box smoke to rise and follow the trail right back to you, unafraid of the flames it could so easily match.

Worshipping Grief

The first time I seen a dead body
I was playing with my cousins in Algeria,
even then, I could not resist the wide desert-plains
beyond a scriptorium of garden gates
and I always roamed too far
with darkness at my tail chasing me back
towards my mother's cry long after sunset.

When we touch the carcass
it is fully enshrouded in clockwork decay.
We keep returning every day more inquisitive,
less disgusted by the poor wild thing
with its cold eye closing in on a jagged thorn.

Death fertilises life, nature's detritus has her own charm;
the pattern of insects over flesh rot to raw-bone,
ossein polished, night after night, by moonlight
as shards and sheens arrived like stilts
for the disappearing clown.

It was funny after all, kids running after each other
in Saharan heat
waving the stench away from their faces
like washing off paint to scream, giggle, delight
at our discovered treasure and well-kept secret.

Each day, a ghastlier deformity held its mantle
until the end of autumn as Samhain snuck in,
when we were greeted by a skeleton,

its beautiful ribcage jutting through grass
an empire now for a few stray ants,
its skull a mirror for the snout of the moon.

The following year, I made my pilgrimage
to face Death again, to check in on finality,
to make sure it wasn't imaginary;
impermanence, mortality and form
as new life had sprouted with flowers brighter
than anywhere else in the field
where sea-air lifted in porous bouts
from erosion's tongue and jetsam gathered
far over the cliff's edge to pay homage
with a helix of shells, a prayer for safe passage.

Blood is only fleeting, vessel is sparse
and gorse is thick to cover what has been left behind,
aborted by time, sullen with nutrient;
Death is composite for new life.
With only one chance at this concept of living;
we live now, we die later
c'est la vie, c'est la mort
as we ourselves fall to our knees in the future,
life lives on; the spectral rain, the sun's rays,
the grief of the plucked-out heart.

Dzifa Benson

For the Love of Hendrik de Jongh, Drummer from Batavia

i

In the beginning,
he was my lord
of the six weeks.
When !Kaub showed
the dark side of his face
again, I had to slough off
my lover's name.

ii

You are on the other side of the water.
Here, my forehead touches only air.
I map the radiant places of your body,
the seams of my skin brittle and ablaze.

iii

Even when the rise and fall of our ribcages insist
we are still here, I try to live above the flood.
I breathe you in. You breathe me out. The world,

in rain-wind and dilate-sun, leans in to learn
which way to carve the howling sweep of years.

iv

You asked: What parts of you are unknown to me?
I answered: This too muchness of self in its not-enoughness.

v

Day empties through us as a Cape sugarbird sparkles
thinly
                                        in the shadows.
You let me follow you into your dreams. Vast night looks
   in,
                                        open-mouthed,
leads us by a nose of buchu into its fluid corners on the
   //Stars Road.
                                        Our eyes don't close.
I want to bury the chameleon of this love in a secret
place   of nerve and sinew
while we wait for the mantis to sing the !Great Hunger
   to sleep.

vi

If I arrived at your voice again would it fatten
      into a new kind of passing time,
pour down my back into this thousand-years
      hollow of my spine? Your memory breathes

warmth over my skin. My body catches it
      like when our astonished spirits
were every crashing leaf on every tree,
      when our hallowed hands cupped
soft curving and fingered lean meat.

vii

You never left. We endured. I was still denied.

viii

My I was him.
In order to live
I had to use
the knife
between us.

!Kaub, //Stars Road and !Great Hunger emulate the click sounds of some South African languages.

Ms Hipson, the tall Dutchwoman, dreams of dancing with a man tall enough to make her feel delicate

I cannot stand silence so it's the glee and the din
of the stage for me. I sway among rafters to the patter
of the gaffer, to the gauge of long drum and hurdy-gurdy.
I am a spiritual sister of giraffe-necked women, daughter
of a stilt-walking Titan. Home is sawdust and greasepaint.
Kin is the spit-snarl of the rabble, half-cut with pale ale.

Ms Sidonia married twice and retired a wealthy woman

God sent me this beard, I will not take it off!
How else would they notice me? This visage
is a lure, toast of the mob, I am a sight to silence
the baying crowd. I cheated death, I fought
and won. That makes me beautiful. I bow now
to the deities who live in my whiskers.

The previous poem and the one above are extracts from a longer sequence entitled *Bartholomew Fair: Natural-born, Man-made & Fake.*

Malika Booker

Points of this Reckoning

1. Outside the poet's window a black and white bird
   stalks the concrete fence daily   like   clockwork.
   His black feathers resplendent against the grey, ageing
   concrete.

2. The poet wonders if this is a symbol and if yes, what is
   the bird symbolic of?

3. What omen is the bird delivering – strutting outside
   the poet's doorstep like a postman?

4. The poet wishes she had the visa to decipher the bird's
   prophesy.

5. The poet reaches out to her dead aunt, wishing she was
   alive with her tea
     leaves, dream   interpretations and answers to every
   sacred message.
   But receives no answer.

6. Today wise Windrush elders like her aunt are dying.
   The news runs amok
     with these disproportionate deaths.

7. The poets heard whispers circulating that these elders harvested dreams of
   phlegm-soaked threads embroidering throats, but
      ignored the literal connotations of these
visions projecting them onto the Windrush deportations (a costly distraction).

8. The citizens marked their homes and those of their carers with orange chalk
   but to no avail. Death suffuses their lungs like
cheese fermenting.

9. The poet marvels at the furtiveness of this virus.
Its pugnacious nature.

10. This phantom made many West Indians in the diaspora sign themselves signing: *duppy know who fi frighten.*

11. The poet notices how the language / proverb is a sort of chameleon, a camouflage,
   or rather (thinking the idea through) how
   circumstances change even the wording of this
traditional
   Jamaican proverb because in these serious times
Duppy move beyond
      frighten to *don't care who fi dead . . .*

12. The poet's sister-in-law is one of the brown-skinned workers whose job has
radically transformed to 'key' – from unappreciated to
homage songs and applause.

13. The poet's sister-in-law states *Brooklyn has the highest body count.* Says *no one collects the bodies, they are told to put the corpse into another room and*
lock the door.
– *Is this the same for the whites* the poet asks.
– The bodies, the bodies – the orderlies are
weeping – fatigued –
so much death.

14. Long ago before funeral parlours West Indians kept their dead bodies at home
and washed
and prepared their dead for burial, someone sat with the body, so it was not
alone. Back then the body was buried quick quick.

15. In Chapeltown policemen circle young black men like rabid hyenas. The poet
watches as at 4 p.m. like clockwork they begin to circle.

16. The poet asks *bird did you come as a messenger about this hunter situation? Is that why you stalk?*
Then the poet apologises,

17. *Apologies bird,* the poet humbly mumbles, *this is my projection onto you . . . I*
beg you grant me a visa to be able to read your vision.

Discordant Mourning

Each morning she drank cocoa tea then swept,
clutching the pointer broom left here by May,
dust and more dust like May's body where she lay,
a burned seed in the muddy soil where worms crept
to feast upon May's flesh whilst she slept.
Our poor strangled brown rabbit, they both say,
wanting to somehow will this past away;
that day wind held back breath whilst fishes wept
and her dresses slipped of off washing lines to fold
into piles onto the bed, where her papa rested his
wretched self, tormented, hand anointing his head
as May, his toughened waterlily, was dead.
Under morning light's gaze, how fragile is
the marriage bed, splintering under death's hold.

Golden Grove

A place scented with the piquant aroma of oranges, so pungent
it tickles our noses. How we would climb the steps into the house
hugged by clusters of leafy trees, whose blossoms scrape the roof
and stroke the outside walls like a lullaby, our fingers caressing skin
as the breeze caused them to dance, and flutter to and fro.
My bare feet on the lacquer floor, then us on the verandah
of my aunt's house, in the hammock rocking, watching the ritual
of nightfall. Bats slinging out of the roofs, winged rats magnificent
in their masses. Black bursts foreshadowing against the fluffy clouds
and a sunset painted sky. How we sat on that verandah and savoured
the night. The crickets and frogs singing with the leaves, me reading
my book on the verandah, leaning back against the glass sliding door
to capture light from the room behind.
This haven for mosquitoes, how palms would slap body parts,
shedding blood in this quiet still. The hum and slaps joining

the chorus of the night. Green coil in the corner, burning red,
then black, before breaking and falling into the tin lid below,
smoke mingling with citrus. My mum and aunt chatting
the language of big women, hushed for prying ears
in the clutch of evening. All is still, watching the dark cloud
descend into charcoal, broken by lights from the neighbour's
windows – lanterns suspended in the darkening street.
How we savoured the night, better yet the blackout power cuts
and the golden flickering glow of the lit kerosene lamps, casting
black smoke up against the unlit window, warring with smoke
from the coil, causing shadows to crawl and dance on the wall.
There is a magic to my aunt's house, even the soft notes of my name
in her mouth like music. In this place where cracked hands hoarded
each shekel, stocking collective coins into a single pile to purchase
this former plantation. How in the land of El Dorado, this treasure
our ancestors had toiled for free, was bought and rechristened
from Williamson to Golden Grove, and now we savour their sacrifices.

How they recast the land into Golden. And when the
seawater ate
the land, eroding the foreshore to expose the seven feet,
burying
the redbrick relics of an old Dutch building – belching
up plates,
mugs, jars and demijohns, relics black with age in this
treasure
grove – we understood how much movement rests here.
Understood
the echo of this history of old times, the sky black coal,
a tangy scent of citrus and a young girl reading the pages
of the night on her aunt's verandah.

Eric Ngalle Charles

Mboa Mi: 'My Country'

you have drowned our gods in white ink.
their screams swallow us.
                    we go

'like the raft of the Medusa'
our houses stand in a sea of tears.
we survive by 'throwing' others overboard.
                    we go.

Heroes

for the Shepherd War Poet, Hedd Wyn
(born Ellis Humphrey Evans, 1887–1917)

Many moons ago
before I was born
a story was told of a great king
called Kuva Likenye.

With tears in his eyes,
Kuva invoked ancient spirits,
they heard his voice,
his lamentations,
they came singing.

'Djembe Kumbi
Eezrewa Etongi
Etongi Ndi Mawongor
Wanna Wa Njuma Ezraweya
Evonda ya Njuma emuka
Ja'ataneya ndo Mavanni'

With the spirits,
Kuva built a wall, a kortoh,
outside the kortoh,
the German war machine raged.

Many moons ago
before morning breeze greeted my face,
a war was fought in a distant land.
It was, as Owen said,

'Dim through the misty panes,
and thick green light
as under a green sea.'

'That old lie.'

In droves they died.
Hedd Wyn went,
a journey of no return.

Beyond the horizon
young boys
young girls
quake in their boots
of what might or might not come
from behind the wall.

Mothers dressed in sackcloth,
picking empty bullet shells,
in reverse.

  In this fight,
  in this great war,
  only the maggots win.

Many moons ago
tales were told of soldiers –
dead and buried in distant lands,
souls roaming,
craving one last journey home.

Hedd Wyn was there,
lost.

They found them dead at dawn,
bodies littered here and there,
holes in their helmets,
one soldier, eyes open
as if following the path of his death.
In his right hand was a note.

'Djembe Kumbi
Eezrewa Etongi
Etongi Ndi Mawongor
Wanna Wa Njuma Ezraweya
Evonda ya Njuma emuka
Ja'ataneya ndo Mavanni'

Translation: This is a war song in the language of the Bakweri/Bantu people from the foothills of Mount Cameroon.

> The djembe is playing loud
> the ezrewa (war gong) sounds
> it speaks of ill winds, danger,
> children of war heed the message,
> the time for war is here,
> let us meet at the border crossing

Kortoh: A protective wall built by Kuva Likenye, the mountain king who mobilised the Bakweri people to resist the German penetration of Buea (one-time capital of German Cameroon 1884–1916) in 1891.

A Song for Freedom

In the furrows of my wrinkles
I carry a picture,
a map,
a flower that never withers.

Under my dragon garments
I hide the scars,
conceal my wounds,
bleeding through cracks of history.

O, neighbours from hills beyond,
we shall draw our borders in poets' ink,
not in blood,
at dawn, before the sunrise,
clutching pictures of our shrines,
we shall march in the rain,
planting seed, singing
'Elizabeth, let our people go.'

Inua Ellams

The Vanishing

Isah's story is that on an evening / thick as crude oil / in a beer parlour overflowing / like the River Niger itself / he heard it whispered / that the mythic thief who only robbed the questionably rich / the legend said to grease the night's hinges / he / who could vanish quick / that nimble finger / his bracelet beaded with human teeth / planned to strip a shipping magnate of his wealth / to drag his capitalist spirit back to the bone-crunching poverty / that gripped the country / Isah's eyes widened like fresh springs and he speed-dialled his boss to double security

Omo's story is that the guards were unconscious / before they hit the ground / he smeared his concoction of blood / brittle leaves and beetle venom across the window bars / murmured sacred incantations and when they parted / like savannah grass / breezed through / like he had done a thousand times before / His landing was soundless as cats' breath / his picking clean as vultures' / his ears keen as sin / until the wife screamed / He hadn't intended violence / but the brave merchant stood guarding her / gripping a knife / which shook / with the danger of inexperience / so he nullified the threat

Regina's story is that she waited days / for her husband's eyelids to part / to catch the twinkleglint beneath his purpled flesh / before she could leave / cross the clogged expressway / to the precinct / to pour out breathlessly the scope of the crime / Only then did she query the sergeant's familiarity / his lithe and limber fingers / that odd bracelet glimmering down his cuff / like a muffled voice / How her lungs shrank / The corners of the office clenched like jaws / Her stomach folded in on its empty self / dropped what seemed a thousand feet / and the ley lines powers that loop through the world / grouped around her like a tightening noose

Of Howling Wolves

When the sister says her colleague's husband came knocking / for his wife / and for the familial in his warm eyes / opened the empty office at dusk / the sky hanging without a question mark / the brother yawns

When the sister describes this husband / parting her / braids splashed against floral wallpaper / the trembling stems / her head pulsing / the loosening belt / the brother is consumed / with an anger he has never known

When he tells his boys / they offer to visit / do the husband the kinds of violence alleys are primed for / One tells of a mob back home / who caught the accused / sliced a thin hole in raw earth / forced consummation / until he bled

When the husband is asked why / he says / he couldn't help it / she led him on / he was drunk / dressed that way she was asking for it / no one had complained before / and / this is what men do

When their fathers agreed / this was true / they were of different eras / these new complaints confused them too / the brother had nightmares / of men like wolves / their jaws bloody / devouring the world / he among them feasting too

A Boy / Twice

After Terrance Hayes and Lauryn Hill

To those taught from childhood / tomorrow is not promised / the end is close as nightshadows / what could dusk falling in late September matter / when my father stops by the bathroom / wondering how much longer I will be / My friend Stephen is dead / he was found earlier / hanging / The loss flows from me like twin streams / Father knocks / unsure what to do / follows as I leave / his hands hovering awkward as lost birds / In my room the streams swell / *Stop crying* he says / he has never seen his son / so sedulously inconsolable / so given to grief / grows impatient as the waters churn ravenous / *Ah ah? What is it! Did you kill him?!* he shouts / as though guilt is the lone inducement for one moved to tears / I fall silent / my streams bricked at their source / and the boy I was who sought his comfort / the son I was to him / I snatch away / to the gulf widening between us / to the drying riverbed / of mangled language and stony bone / and bury for years

Let me begin again / To those who learn late in life / tomorrow is not promised / the end is close as nightshadows / dusk falling in late September explains everything / hands awkward as lost birds / a father's ravenous impatience / In taking Stephen / Death slid its glacial fingers through the neckskin of our family / stirred me wild / drove Father to harsh pronouncements / In 2007 a blood vessel ruptured / in this man's brain / drowning him within himself / Think Death / again stirring / his grey matter to red swamp / In the hospital / he tried to rise off his bed and swayed / like a loosened mountain / His pyjamas slipped revealing / his full shrivelled length / he crumbled to tears / melting all the sureties I held of the world / I rushed to help / we blurred / limb to limb / flesh to flesh / skin to primordial soup of dulled synapses / damp stars / sweatwater / tangled muscle / tears like twin rivers flowing back and forth afresh / We collapsed to the floor / splashed out / glistening as if calves from the same womb in morning light / then staggered up slowly to our knees / our feet / shaking / shaken / Should you ever meet and share this story / tell him again / I too was born

Samatar Elmi

[Etymologies]

i. Albion

Albion, as in Al Bayoon, the in-between
is all I hear when you scream at me
from across the parapet. Bayoon
you and I, this stitch of browning turf
is Albion, soaked and distending.
And bayoon the earth and the sky –
rainbows that may or may not appear
bayoon our faintly whispered losses.

Albion, as in purgatory, or perhaps
an oasis, or mirages in the sand,
which itself is the cruellest state in limbo;
to think for a moment that the in-between
could be anything but Albion,
could be anything but a home.

ii. Gauls

I think of concentric circles, Vercingetorix,
a siege within a siege ad infinitum
until the distinctions between them,

a caesar and a chieftain,
is reduced to shades of echoes,
between the wings of moths.

Gaul, somewhere about the guts, stomach
for a fight that can't be won, as in *kaala*
gaal, 'black foreigner' in her land of birth,
as in bile, yellow belly, as in coward,
the gall to run and run in circles,
and the balls to settle down, here

this hallowed, hollowed out home
that crept up and swallowed everything.

The Fear

after Miguel Algarín

i.

Sometimes I fear crossing the ever-so-thin line
such is the fear I daren't look down
like Blodin and Petit, except my crutch
can barely hold its own, a crushed roach
rolls and I can taste both it and the lips
that pursed and paused.
I juggle these doubts and witness
the years it takes from the slip.
In this milieu, a single misstep
will vagabond you.
Sometimes I spot the same glint in my son's eyes
and all I hear is crashing water
our bodies falling out of the sky.

ii.

Sometimes, along the quayside, my son
walks up ahead unburdened
and I know I must have walked like this –
a skater on a frozen lake.

I take this picture and store it
in place of the memory that time
or smoke or a knock on the head
rubbed until erasure
– it happens quicker in Eurasia.

One day, I'll wonder
how I came to watch my gliding self
through the eyes of my father –
out of body, out of mind.

Sometimes, along the quayside, we pass
a fellow burning. I go to pinch my nose
but it's too late. I am inhaled
in the trail of smoke, a tail
wags the head and lifts the dead by inches.
I am stopped, here, in other dimensions.
And I can't see how far my son
will jolly on for.

Coda

They had changed their throats and had the throats of birds
– W. B. Yeats

The signal is given for an angel
to draw a cold breath, lips pursed
on the brass mouth of a horn
that spans the glacial width
of measurement itself
– we brace ourselves, for a note
that will cut through the air
like shrapnel, a signal to roll back
the black rug of the world.

A white ancestor calls me to Ypres.
He has waited, this boy of seventeen
waited, while the long line of boys
has barely budged in a hundred years,
he does not wait with them,
but for one of his own to conduit
the taste of iron and innocence
mixed with scattered salt
– he can't get the acid off his tongue
while he searches for lemon trees
on these fields of ritual sacrifice,
son of my grandson he says

you will feel the moment
the gates are closing

by the muffling of the ears
and distance.

And some of us can sense
a tension in the ribbons that bind us,
a weariness in the angels
that bring our infants to laughter,
while the imperceptible movement
of the small hand ticks along.
And some of us are resigned
that nothing good can come
from either the deadly pitch

or our deathly silence.

Khadijah Ibrahiim

Herman Avenue Hand-Cart Woman

Old miss lady black skin shine
like the inside of one full cocoa basket

lush Jamaica
wearing a washed-out sky-blue sun cap
ripe sorrel-red skirt and torn blouse
with flowers
of the island

she walks Herman Avenue
with ease selling callaloo

from a homemade hardtime-style
handcart – worn down
pram wheels – steel wire n hinged
n lean off

knowing
every pothole n crack
in de road n sidewalk chat

the mid-morning swells
and hisses with water hoses
along the avenue

slakes
dried soil and sun-burnt grass

sweat pours resurrects her
dragging flip-flop soles – resembles
her handcart's wheels

she drags n treads
winding hips in her take-your-time
syncopated tempo
like driftwood

melodies
afloat on rock n water
to a pitched alto

callaloo – pak-choi – okra
callaloo

her voice
cuts a Sunday Sankey
song on repeat

callaloo – pak-choi – okra
callaloo

she stops at number 403 – drinks ice water
rinses the sweat from her face

brings back the shine-black
of her body –

to mash daily chat of wha' gwarn ah town
the labrish n kurra kurra

push up plum-lips – kiss-teeth at
the price of tings

revels in
who's a teef
who gwarn ah foreign?
what Miss so and so dry foot boy
did the other day –
who a sells good breadfruit

she steps n
snaps to free flow with her cart

callaloo – pak-choi – okra

callaloo

callaloo

two hundred dollars – see me here
mi ave callaloo – pak-choi – okra

callaloo

callaloo

Hey miss!
you have some pak-choi

Miss Lady!
Mi noh have none
last one just sell

see de nice callaloo
two hundred dollars

pak-choi – pak-choi done

mi ave callaloo – okra

callaloo

callaloo

mi ave

callaloo
callaloo
callaloo

Bath Prescription 1

eh eh . . .

'See an blind, hear an def'

is why
nobody wants to talk
it . . .

the bush-bath thing
the work of the healer's yard

is the space
between knowing, and
the silence of tongues – that oscillate
above island faith

the mother of the healer's yard
witnesses those who come and go

the work of Obeah

Myal science some say!

it . . .

is buried in old time rituals

some just hush mouth
because of fear

or pretend to make Jesus a friend

'what a friend we have . . .'

a god born out of a stinking past
of old Massa Ra'tid whip n lash ways /

disembodied – African – Mulatto – Indian
rites /
Criminalised

it . . .

Drum 'n' Kromanti
dust out of salty skin / just knowing

it . . .

is the reason why silence
stutters / dead quite

but

it . . .

is the yard of night healing

altar of
remedies / preserved in bush yard
plants n ground spirit works
All come for ritual bathing / some are dipped
like Bedward

benevolent / god / like face

to wash out sleepless troubles
voices possessed / in de rudeness
of duppy / sucking stones
hot breath
blown in from
darkness

all seek it / each release
none claim

it . . .

This
bath preparation
a sacred healing
prescribed
in de Mother's yard.

Bush Craft Prescription

To cleanse the home
of rotten duppy

the dead who were never tied down at
the burial ground

the dead who left / coffin / bed /

the dead who turn watchful / over the living /
the dead who vex to rass

the dead who find ways / to roam
throw stones / suduçe and sex u

the dead who come with the rawness of eggs
and the stink of shadows

if / if / u
are not afraid to call up old folk lyrics / circle
tuff ground / and
shape the night sky
drum out rhythm

sweep clean
wash it / holy

Buy a new tin pan
When night falls take the pan
to the sea, fill with water

from a fresh wave coming to shore
recite Psalms 23
turn anti-clockwise

return home, don't look back
don't speak,
trust no shadow after dark

If someone calls to you
don't answer

drop plenty of sticks and stones to the ground
to lead de dead / into confusion
as a matter / of ritual
tie a piece of red cloth around a broomstick
hang it in a tree

step backwards / into your home
wash the floor / add High John the conqueror
mop up / return it back to the
sound of sea waves

listen . . .
dead frequency / moves
weightless / duppy / recur

repeat 3 time
as prescribed . . .

Keith Jarrett

My mother sings of how she got her education

at the cross, she catch wise,
like the cedars of Lebanon
and speak King James English   good good
how you mean seh you cyaan understan?

Him whom have hears to ear
        mek him ear
and he whom cyaan ear mus feel
Babylon throne mus fall

Blessed is the old-time religion
it was good for Paul and Silas
it was good for Snoop and Stormzy
it was good for Chance the Rapper

it was good for my mother
good for my father
so it's good enough for me.

Scalp

Receding since twenty-four, I think of all the thin-
skinned prophets
with thinner hair, how, in other circumstances, I might
have been President
(the midwife who delivered me – according to my
mother –
said I cried like a leader) or inherited a double portion of
the Spirit.

It's a myth that male pattern baldness runs in the mother's
genes.
Her father died with a full head of grey; I will die with
my cap on.
I don't recognise myself in the mirror without one and,
except for one
moment of lucidity in the yard, my granddad didn't
recognise me, either.

When teaching, I get called far worse than *baldy*. I
wouldn't wish for my pupils' deaths
although II Kings 2 ends with two she-bears mauling
the prophet Elisha's young tormenters.
In the King James version, they say *Go up, thou bald head!*
It's funny as hell
then it isn't. They're not even named. Forty-two kids
killed at God's bidding.

Since becoming a full-time faggot, I've been rethinking
power imbalances,

all the strands that tie structural oppressions together.
When I was a child,
handing my mother her rollers, one by one, at night, I didn't question God
this way. And then one day, I became too old to be so close to her parted scalp.

I still don't question my mother – or rarely. This, I would venture, does run
in our genes; her mother was twice as spirited. I peel my head every fourth
day with a zero-fade clipper. Less hair lands on the bathroom floor each time
– a mixed blessing. Though I now seldom pray, I call her more, trying to let go.

Nor the Arrow That Flies in the Day

parakeets possess a particular morning restlessness
that shifts my weight from foot to foot as I wait
by the kettle-side   observe their green crests
bobbing in and out of the fourth-floor drain holes
of the high-rise opposite   pans clang in the flat above
and I submit to this intrusion   with the patience of—
I share my father's name and faded hair and wanderi—
hear them skit— do they play? do they live day to day
in the way that the well-rehearsed bible verse proclaims?

no matter   here we mind our business because density
demands discretion of us   and there is no such thing
as community   with only two exceptions:
a) you own wings or b) you walk with a thing that barks
so we remember faces but rarely exchange names
I know what to shout to my downstairs neighbour's pet
I'm damned if I can call out to her child   not sure
if this is on   where have the restless parakeets gone?

what sounds like it should be a threat? *the water is*
  troubled
my appetite's whet   I'm vexed to share my father's
  want
of ritual   coffee first   or in his case switch out
coffee for *God*   or *God* for *control* or— speaking of
  terrors
I am certain I share my father's face in this particular
  light
and it is dark and the water warms and I lift my eyes

and am grateful not to have feared the rapture since—

does steam dream of heaven while catching ceilings?
if mould could testify it would speak of its abundance
its nurturing power its anointing   if you will allow
this brief embellishment   of course you must
in this poem it's my window and my crockery
but of course   it is correct to share   pull up a pew

in this poem the kettle is a shade of green so satisfactory
so fitting for this foggy and automatic ritual of renewal
and here I am a child   or rather a kettle   filled
with the spirit of morning   or switch out the pans
clanging above for trumpets   or in this poem
  someth—

switch the *or*s for ampersands and observe it multiply
do not question the impertinence of birds or neighbours
or my father's hands   which are my
  hands   hovering
beside the handle   laying hands   the bubbling

it goes without sa—   why I must stand by to oversee
why I must not allow it to come to the boil—look, flapping!
see   the young   rose-ringed parakeets of London

how their foreflappers   escaped   from captivity
how   dense   they must wing   how I must   pour

steam   fly   free

Anthony Joseph

Naming

To name something is to wait for it
in a place where you think it will pass.
– Amiri Baraka

Something about how we have names for everything.
How each leaf has its place at the shaded side of the river,
the dark dirt under the cocoa onion, has a name
for that kind of soil. The soft
    cup of scales
forming the echeveria
    has a name,
the way it folds. The filament
in the light of the firefly – the wick, the tail
has a name –
    luciferin, in the production of light.
Water on the knee and it has a name
– meniscus – effusion
which is really, a form of
    liquid textology –
    dividing the meat into chunk and gill.

Once
there were still unseen places and things,
corners of experience which had no name,
and so you could walk upon them
and meet them solid for the first time
be dubwise and dread and hail them up
and bump locks head.
Dread.

And my grandmother said
that if the flying frog leapt
and landed on your face, or the soft
fold of your arm,
that it would stay there,
attach itself
as if with glue
and you would have to
iron or steam steel, impress
upon the frog-back skin till it stick to the stainless heat,
until it release
an' peel off.

We returned from country visits, from visiting kin or churches
hid in bush to find: flying frogs, perched in corners of the house.
Trapped in their silence of peace, I never saw their leap.
But I seen what hurricanes could do to islands.
I seen it on TV and it had a name.

Nigropalmatus,
Hylidae,
Rhacophorus
– fringe-limbed or marvellous –
Ecnomiohyla
Polypedates

– in the calabash tree
– where it has a name.

My cousin Alvin and the hillside
where bananas are grown from seed.
This place has a dance, and it has a name,
even vinegar has a seed.
We were wild
children.
We had names with which we
moved through space
like blades.

Wire, God of Wallerfield

: somnambulist of trees :
: barbed like afro-headed wire :
                    – lingering –
            torn – wire – god
who ran away from the orphanage
from iron bridge rust red
hid beneath: a hollow stream: must be
river fish   :   razor grass
            Wallerfield
                    weed
Bore brutal fruit, truth in earth too dry
to give life, brittle green
guava: trees:
– their velvet grain:
            Caribbean gothic –
            Catholic sin:
to sleep: in sin thick as shade as
the hog plum tree, peep
– the salt, lick
            spinning in barren land
            between the highway
            and the blue
            Valencia

            river.

House Party, Mt Lambert, 1978

for Tanty Virgin and Champ in Malick

One turntable was all DJ Champ had.
The fade was to wait.
Two big speaker box for the boom.
                    Two tweeters
hung like bees on wire above the front door.
        Sacred-hearted Jesus
Mister Clarence dancing to Lord Nelson's 'Night Train'
was the only glimpse we stole of him in this motion:
decorous, with his head up and easy,
smiling even, holding out his glass
of Whiteways of Whimple
to the side so it don't spill
when he slide and spin on his heel.
There were full women in the kitchen smoking
filterless Broadways. Is hard scotch they sipping.
Tanty Ursula was young then, among them, strong
and long before her stroke, bosom tough and hair jet black –
Ursula had plenty verve.
She would stand unsolicited and sing to the room.
Sing out with her tremulous voice. Sing, 'My Way'
or 'Evergreen', wavering between keys but upwards she drove,
into the wild arc
            of her highest note.

Safiya Kamaria Kinshasa

Bitch Ghazal

fleeing to a less hairy duvet, he screams *come back bitch*
my best friend has stopped panting, I turn an' scream *get up bitch*

LA, third city I survived hiding under tables
joined Kendrick singing back at Ms Nature *ya bish ya bish*

doan keep 'im waitin' fuh 'im money, dat palm stay thirsty
even if 'im say he need you an' you de bottom bitch

a few boys chilling at the corner were mauled by police
how the cop mentored the mongrel's mouth, now they fear the bitch

this Ms didn't try too hard with Black kids, ignored our hands
new girl next to me stopped trying, scraped B-I-T-C-H

back it up too good an' thick you risk forgettin' your name
she wiped it over a man's crotch, left Rick's club a bad bitch

Saf-ya Cam— ri Cam— Shit— Kin-sa, are you in the right room?
I, Safiya Kamaria Kinshasa, work here BITCH . . .

Hurricanes Also Taught Us How to Be Sophisticated When Things Get Messy

Barbados, 2002

her seven-inch Ṣàngó's gut de crops
epaulettes widowed tin from shacks

i remember de shade from de brim of her hat
a fine fine tilt, flashin' a spike-toothed smile

sashayin' wit' Sunday evenin' liquor in her hips

those who failed to flee got rouched at de seams
dragged like a wedding veil down Swan Street

powerlines nicked loose stiches
crystals tripped out her thigh

a whole island drippin' in rocks

when she finally strut her way into fatigue
de sun pressed its paw prints on de catwalk

she was floatin' like nain happen
like her torn dress was de way it was s'posed to look

her filth looked pretty pretty dribblin' down de runway

Slow Whine

,

: ,

– .

/

.

,

!!!

,

!

:

, –

.

,

!!!!!

.

!!!!

Vanessa Kisuule

Auntiehood

It
is not,
nor was it ever,
about the crass fact of blood.
There's aunts and there's *aunties*.
Diaspora kids heed the difference,
just-so ratio of hip to metronome earring.
Sometimes but not often your father's sister,
more likely your mum's scorned but grudgingly
favoured friend, some uncle's not-so-secret mistress
turned community seer sat in the sagging sofa's mouth
gossip drunk, hips waterfalling from jeans,
slander on another auntie visits her tongue,
leaves oily stains on the 'Persian' rug.
If you have to ask if she is or isn't,
she's not. Know that auntiehood
can't be forced or coaxed
into the spirit, one day
you are summoned,
refashioned in
kissed teeth
and razor
tut.

Blessings

She says your arms look flabby in vest tops.
Picking fluff from your afro she frowns, asks
what kind of name is that for a boyfriend?

You are told to serve her cold juice in
a tall glass, greet her on bent knees
as if seeking blessings or forgiveness.

She throws a glance at you,
sharp and private as toothache.
You refill her glass only when asked.

She leans her weight into fresh stories
of cousins you've met at christenings
a blur of beaded braids, buck teeth and satin.

One is pregnant, another studying Medicine,
one sent to Kampala with no return ticket,
cheek no doubt still stinging.

You take the empty glass away and
in silence slice her up.
Birth-bombed stomach. The stupid way

she pronounces 'develop', swallowing the O.
Her fat husband and rude daughter.
Bulbous mole on her shoulder, a sickened pearl.

Her whole face a pursed knuckle.

The oily stew she made when you
stayed at her house for what felt like years
but was a week, your mother stuck or sick

or gone for good, they never said.
She held you like her own that first night,
the next day the scowl had returned.

Her bunions. The tacky silver clasp
on her knock-off shoes. You make of her a
Brixton butcher's window. And with no hindsight

to smite you, you sponge the glass clean
of plum lipstick. You hear her on the stairs,
telling a story that breaks your mother open
with laughter.

On Freezing A Dead Son

Brute boy. Twitch lip. Clear braces.
Never showed teeth in school photos.
No sadder than other sad boys

who seemed to pull through, grow
beards, make babies with sweet girls
and name them after country singers.

After, she saw the word *death*
flanked with quotation marks and her
breath left her lips in one long whistle.

It's a choice, after all. Her son knew that
more than most. Ha. Suicide is a joke
too impatient for the punchline.

The room grew dark as she scrolled
past page three, four and five of Google,
untamed tundra where strange things live,

grief so ravenous it eats God in one bite,
wiping its mouth with fifty-dollar bills.
What is hope but a moment or a man

paused in its prime, a bribe slipped inside
a casket. The last time she glowed like this
she was pregnant and addicted to ice.

Her husband would drive five miles to
find the right kind that crunched like gravel.
Ice ice baby, they giggled, the image
thrilling them immensely.

Rachel Long

Your Daddy Ain't Rich

but you can swipe his card from his wallet
for a few bits on eBay, without him noticing
till his statement swoops down onto the mat.

The month you realised it arrived the same time
as your period, it became easy to intercept it.
You don't take the piss, you understand what a
  mortgage is

to people like your parents, hard-working, yeah, I get it.
I've got a bone to pick with you, he'll say in your bedroom
  doorway
every few months, when you haven't been fast enough

I've got a bone to pick with you, he says
the same thing each time, like it's the same bone,
meek, mere, like the one in the ear

or the one in your little toe,
that won't heal if you jam it
into a wall and break it. Nothing much anyone
  can do.

It was just a few bits, clothes mostly, jeans
to catwalk into the common room,
ripped and in a smaller size each time.

And what's this here. What sort of jeans cost this much?
Dad nudges his glasses up, holds his statement to the light.
Oh, that was a one-time purchase

– Petrol blue with the huge brass padlock. Oh! that bag
was worth sitting on the hard chair
at the family computer while they were all eating dinner

and bidding on it, and bidding on it. That bag was worth
risking all the small bones for
when you have a daddy who will only pour

more and more ice water
into the bucket
at your feet.

As If

I miss your hands on me, your mouth. Earlier
I missed you in the honey aisle – we haven't even
been grocery shopping yet but I want to
be en pointe in the kitchen, open the highest
cupboard, set the things you like inside;
white bread, long-life cow's milk. I even bought
instant coffee and refrained from informing the cashier
that it wasn't for me, woman of refined taste.
Who am I kidding? I'd buy you a sack of rice
and lug it back on my head. I don't even hate
admitting this. I've forgotten what I once did
before I glowed in search of slippers.
If you don't like your feet touching the floor,
they don't have to anymore.

Adam Lowe

Desire

The girl opposite me on the train had stars carved in her tights. She was reading *American Psycho*
and blushing. You could see Christian Bale on her lips, the taste of cheese, the gnaw of outrageous
desire. And I was on my way to *him*. She was buried in the pages of murder, and I was dreaming –
buried in the cheeks of his flesh. The bitter-sweat stench of old cannabis lingered from the man
beside me. He was acrid, but right now I tasted sweet. Desire is a funny thing – creeps in when you
least expect it, runs off without warning, and rarely stays put. It's unwelcome. It arrives in the rain
and the snow and sun, and stays as long as it wishes. It's a bad houseguest that never does the dishes
– only smashes them while claiming to dance. But I can't find the right excuses to turn it away
from the doorstep. I always step aside for those men who stink of risk. I get it wrong too many
times but to get it right once – that is the trick – and to do it at all tastes so sweet. I wanted to press
my lips to his armpits. Taste the tang there in the dip. Then run my tongue in waxing waves over the

stretch of his belly. I wanted to sit on him, let him sink in
and taste the shapes of his mouth. The girl
across could smell the desire reeking like booze or m-cat
from me. She could feel it pulsing and
writhing. She blushed deeper. The air had become my
bloodstream. Soon I would arrive. I could
smell the green syrupy weed in my pocket. I was peeling
the thick, river taste. The conductor
charged past, now aflame with purpose. Nothing to do
with me. Sleek train gliding through throat of
night – I'm coming – I'm coming for you. Can you take
me in the grip of your salty arms and make
me feel girded – make me feel whole? The time is almost
upon us. Can you feel it? How does it
feel? The darkness slid aside as train pulled itself into
station, away from the night. I was following
a trail of you. Could smell that musky, malty squint of
your arsehole, rippling round my tongue. A
concertina of flesh. Yes! I could – can still – taste you. The
fruit of you has found me again, even now.

Aftermath

In the aftermath, I couldn't set foot in the bar.
The first time I tried, I broke open in a fit of tears.

Your puppy fat and wet kisses, your nibble on my bottom lip.
Reaching down to meet the stiffness, too tired, I decline.

Hysterical, I couldn't look him in the eye for all
the torment he'd made me feel: that it was my fault,

With head full of cocktails and arms leaden with sleep,
I try to roll away, but you slip yourself back in.

that no one would believe me, that no to him
meant yes, that even as I tried to sleep in a friend's bed,

Then you stop, I feel relieved, ready to slip off back to sleep,
and the dark ready to claim me. Only to be pierced again . . .

I could find no rest. And it showed me the tyranny
of lust, the marble ceiling weight of sex above,

Jolted out of night's comfort, the sheets are raw against my skin.

I can smell the stink of spirits on you, your
insistence, your rage.

a crushing blanket, a body rolled onto me that won't
budge,
the spear of your intrusion a nagging question that won't
wait

When I leave in the morning, I am thick with grief,
confusion
and shame. I fog over on the details, sometimes even
your name.

for an answer even in the dead of night. And still,
I can't bring myself to blame you in the aftermath.

Once We Were Wolves

dashing like smoke through silvered firs.
Our eyes were hurtling moons in the violence
of night, affixed upon our prey of hare and hart.
Our bodies were frosted pine needles, the shadowy
grace of fear. Our paws made the silent tread
not of feet but of rampant years. Our muzzles
described scree-paved landslides, and our fangs
were the jagged treetops in misty midnight.
Our tails, meanwhile, saluted heaven like our
looning cries. We had wilderness for comfort,
the hunt for our joy, and the rain that found us
stirred the taste of earth from beneath our claws.

Nick Makoha

An Essay on Man

Maybe the measure of life's brief sequence
can be found in the mist that hangs over trees
as their branches twist in the wind. A jealous
fire ploughs through an abandoned warehouse
and pays no attention to the security guard.
His dead eyes widening betray their duty.
Everything floods in. His ex-wife wonders
how it happened. The policemen at the door
ask for a glass of water. Biting her top lip,
she lets the evening in and offers them broken
rice with fried chicken and coleslaw. As the stars
appear, with their mouths full of food, the clock
will chime. Despite the heat of the day they
eat the meat to the bone. You are right to ask
the question. Why share the favourite meal of
the man she once loved? Let me place before
you one or two things; the eye hungers for what
it can't find, a wave of delivery trucks roar to
a stop. She throws a window open, puts on his
old coat and takes a drag from a cigarette a lady
would not smoke. If it wasn't for the fence you
would see her out on the porch tucking her hair

behind her left ear, holding the smoke that fits
inside her body. What does she need it for?
It is the last wave of the man who lived inside her.

Pythagoras Theorem

$a^2 + b^2 = c^2$

a^2

Remember that summer when
edges went? The whole night
became concentrated darkness,
a neon moon against a pitch sky
(not enough to light the backboard).
Bills not paid but we were up by
two in the third game of the best of seven.

b^2

Their point guard calling an illegal pick
as we double-teamed, breathing like dogs
on a leash. I was staying in the spare room
of your house. Living below the line
like denominators until I learnt algebra:
from the word *al-jabr* – the reunion
of broken parts. Your nephew, the third man,
floated by (a silver shadow) and drained
a three crunch through the chains.

c^2

His motto, *Those who lack the courage*
will always find a philosophy to justify it.
It is a state of being unrestricted.
My wife's fortnightly child-support cheques
last three weeks. All numbers are divisible
by one: the act of being divided. Isn't the God

of the Hebrews also the God of Islam?
We are at right angles the sum of each other.
And then there is zero (that empty place),
where heat and light are meaningless.

The Long Duration of a Split Second

Umm al-Hiran, 2017

Because all language lacks fluency in this pretence the sky
itself was wilderness.
A camera with its crooked frame was the first eye
searching for answers. In this
margin of the day, a helicopter unsure of how to get out
of the world glided down
through cloud cover and became a second infrared eye. Its
purpose to separate
people from trees and hills, still warm with the day's heat,
from the shadows. Men dressed
for war used torches like fireflies to follow the echoes.
Inside a whisper – revenge,
inside revenge – a language – inside the language – an
algorithm of how to turn a collage
of startling images into a village of some importance. A
car horn shrieked like an unfed
child to introduce the theory of infinite endings. Within
that horn an eruption and within
that eruption an another. Then fourteen seconds of
darkness – before the camera

reproduced men in the motion of battle.

He who conforms to loss of land must be
the right enemy. It is easier to divide the
world this way. A disobedient tribe explain
their extinction in the desert. To begin the
story again, what was once a village on a

rock they will call it Jerusalem. But who
discovered you? Outside the thermal frame,
a woman's voice cries after four gunshots
made visible by a cloud of hot air invent a
new kind of time. Paradise and violence are
the same road, one cannot exist without
the other, both gladly accept loss. A bullet
has found its currency spiralling up towards
a moving vehicle whose engine has died.
Getting away is what a road is for. A car
door opened to the wilderness and so this
hill became a portrait of death. A fatal
bullet turned the driver the shape of
someone else as the flowers are blamed
themselves.

Karen McCarthy Woolf

from **Unsafe**

electric enactments
    & contractions
    first on cattle & then
    in camps, camps they
        entangled & snared

        in wars: Boer, One, Two & so forth
    each iteration more intense
        & sphincter-like contracted out
                to architects & engineers

in the camps, camps
            entangled & snared

it is testament, as in testes, as in testosterone, as in test
to make static
to immobilise, in a military sense
to design & follow
a procedure, always a procedure
orders, in an order

& that procedure in this case being America's Homestead Act
& that procedure being the wire as assailant, as asterisk
& that this asterisk was emphatic
& that this asterisk was both legislative & actual
& that this asterisk was intentional & genocidal

& that the procedure was with precedent
(& to be explicit
as it is necessary, still, to be explicit)
                on indigenous bodies, on black bodies,
                on brown bodies, on child bodies, crammed in

crammed to fit—crammed
landless bodies of the poor
crammed in, thrown off, claimed for
crammed underneath, choked, held landless
& evicted

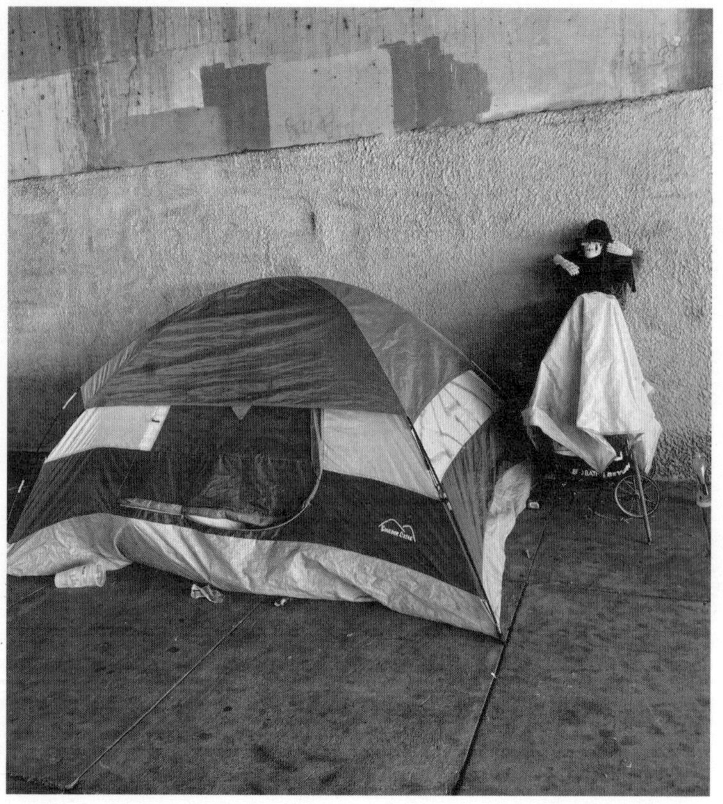

& it is painful, this exile from the garden. Of the house.
With a witch—

I am burning sage at the edges of a doorway, sage
from the plains, plains I remember in a waking dream, plains

I have barely driven through, plains
        where the land is closer to the sky, where
        the sky is imminent.

Sage from an English garden, sage
        my mother taught me—

Momtaza Mehri

A Comparative History of Fire

aflame   aflush   whole hearts   aflutter
    we are undone
cleansed with new meaning (if only for this moment)
    if only for ourselves
hope-snatching & dutty
    boukman's prayer at bois (a girl can dream)
we are liquid-limbed   sparking the ground under our feet
    bathing in the bathos between digital mo(u)rnings
& bookmarked recipes
    neither meme nor mammy
our sisters are slick-braided & afoot
    erzulies of the ends   of the endless
tart taste of summer swells their tongues
    they pose with the fresh carcass of a police car
Wish You Were Here!
    riot as postcard
as historical post-date
    bury your demands as soon as they are made (post-haste)
flamecaster fatimans   we mourn who you have had to be
    teach the poets what poetry is

what it could be   bussa bussa
    buss case (case being the world)
being the condition
    being the contours of mass misery
moving   always moving
    masked & gorgeously inadequate
ancestors file their manicured nails
    shoot dice   share bad jokes
eat perfectly round peaches
    they have earned the right to be left alone
the luxury of choosing
    when to strike   & when to rest
watch us watch crackling screens
    in peeling alleyways   from our lonely lodgings
our parochial plantations   our respective babylons
    unfreedom is so boring
we bear it like ants tortured by cruel children
    an ugly brooch of an inheritance
a lit match licks the lip of a field
    by its light   we undress all pretensions
what others call our worst is usually our best
    we own everything we can see
& nothing we can touch

hooyos

dragged up into other languages hooyos who didn't speak english swedish german finnish dutch hooyos who could read in arabic but couldn't understand bottle-throwing egyptian nor accented humiliation hooyos who didn't speak at all hooyos with no use for niceties hooyos with dreams of their own hooyos who debilitated us with the weight of their dreams hooyos who married high-school sweethearts hooyos who married bus drivers hooyos who married unrepentant killers hooyos who sang for them hooyos who lent a soundtrack to slaughter hooyos by blood hooyos by loose association hooyos by archipelagos of clan hooyos by name hooyos by namelessness hooyos unmoored mothering milk-froth memoried maladjusted mariin mamas who stalk the hallways of our poems are gracious enough to pretend we are more than desperate ventriloquists more than humane cannibals hooyos we did not ask but you gave   what we asked for   you couldn't

Even on Canvas, Oilfields Burn

for Layla Al-Attar

denied / a visa to her own exhibition / on downy wings
/ her paintings left / without her / they had their papers
/ her lapful of ashes / would only hold them back /
euphrates ever-ebbing / ebbs / bears witness to more
than what any / body / of water / should / what does
not change / reminds us of all that has / if it clings to
the banks / it has its valid reasons / she spins at the feet /
of full-lipped sumerian kings / watch this teardrop hang
gorgeously / she will live / in its circular promise /
forgive us for preferring / the bronze tyrants of our
yesterdays / the desperate can't be blamed / for their
bedtime stories / mourn what has never truly existed /
until you are sure that it did / once /

a life spent breaching dams of documentation / she
holds head in hands / palms flooded with revised histories
/ the angels of modernisation carried you / to moscow
blossoms / to adeni afternoons / watched over these
unprotected children / of former protectorates / the
mandated upon / adrift without mandate / with only the
miscellany of their grief / inheritors of pooled betrayals /
salt mines of apathy / backdrops of black flags & muddied
skies / we gift you the descriptors we use / to blunt our
calculated cruelty / lovingly handpicked euphemisms /
swirled in the bouquet / of our bloodied mouths / *general
purpose* bombs / *bouncing* bombs / *guided* bombs / *smart*
bombs / like boisterous children running the length / of
al mutanabbi street / their falling hail of giggles /

colouring the night air / how do you measure the intelli-
gence of a bomb? /

by who it chooses / by who it knows it can choose again
/ & again / by its disavowal of origin / by its tally of
collateral / stray goats / weeping seraphims / white-
throated partridges / bruised peaches / al amiriyah /
orphaned schoolbooks / wild tarragon / myths are the
only shelters we can afford / we refuse / to recognise our
reflections / grace is a yawning woman in a foreign
country / sweeping the cracked stoop / of her new home
/ learning / each morning / to live with what it has
done / what it does / to her old one / trying to keep /
the frayed hem of her dress / as clean as her hands /

Bridget Minamore

Golden Shovel for My People

after Margaret Walker

This is where it started: I have been searching for
a new way of living breathing thriving but my
body has begun to fill with broken people /
The sounds they make feel infinite / Everywhere
I look – in each of my dark corners – I see singing /
I see masses marching searching hunting for their
new world, the home they knew each so-called slave
should would could be entitled to / And their solemn
   songs
are choking me / I have repeatedly
asked begged demanded this noise stop but their
mouths are taped open, their hands frozen – some dirges
need conducting; are too cold to let go of easily – and
I have been sitting inside myself with their
music bobbing like bad boats / Their ditties
on green repeat / Do I feel envy? At the assurance and
acceptance only the long-dead feel? / Music is licking my
   ears, their
knowledge knows nothing but the blues
but that is all they need / Meanwhile I know whites and
we all know that's the problem / These songs last jubilees

and it's obvious I can't keep praying
for silence for an indefinite period of time / Their
music is a reminder to stay angry / My prayers
cannot hear themselves amongst the nightly
cacophony of my ancestors / My body wants to
be empty but it is full of black shards, it is an
example of yet another known unknown /
I wonder if the long-gone who haunt me think I am a
god /
I should kneel at my own altar but I tried bending
and lost my balance and now I can't stand up / Their
racket might be exhausting but when they sing my knees
refuse to knock /   This is how it ends: I humbly
request an audience with my own black body / I want to
search for new ways to live amongst the noise / I am an
item of measurement I cannot understand / My people
are unseen /
They are inside me / The music scares holds hurts / You
/ Give me power

Catching Joke

I try to make him laugh
when I see him

when I see him
I see all black men

I see all black men
suffering

suffering
like sadness sits on skin

like sadness sits on skin
like darkness, like light

like darkness, like light
my skin is a smooth surface

my skin is a smooth surface
my skin became hard

my skin became hard
like a painful disease

like a painful disease
I can't breathe, and

I can't breathe, and
I have stopped watching the news

I have stopped watching the news
it hurts

it hurts
he will die one day

he will die one day
like all black men

like all black men
my life is fragile

my life is fragile
round here

round here
it's like a snake

it's like a snake
bulbous with bodies like ours

bulbous with bodies like ours
it's swallowing

it's swallowing
something black

something black
something black

something black
like we are

like we are
the ones killing things

the ones killing things
like us

like us
they are

they are
ignoring everything

ignoring everything
I try to make him laugh

Sestina for Kara Walker

Nevertheless, I know that we are Black;
held in skin that shouts   remember.
I know many do not listen. I know many witness
pain but do not see the roots of it, I know we water
it regardless so it grows, and still I know our Blackness is
   a gift
and doesn't hurt the way they think it does. I know I am
   a daughter

of the land my parents left. I know I am a daughter
that has pride in borders forged in fire. Perhaps we Blacks
are alchemists, melting the metal of our trauma into gifts.
My second passport claims one country, so I pretend I
   don't remember
my mother's mother considered the place across the water
– where my father's father lived and died – a separate
   state. Witness

this: I am ignoring tiny truths in the name of faux-unity. I
   am witness
to the way we sons and daughters
of the new world hold our parents' countries close.
   We water-
dwelling wendigos; perhaps if the black
of my body eats itself I will remember
to be greedy because the presence of us here is a gift.

My parents and I are alive in this country and it is a gift.
My grandmother lived long enough to witness

me stop trying to learn her language. I remember
her eyes watching her seventh child's only daughter's
closed mouth. I know she was not ashamed because
despite the black
of my skin I was and still am a foreigner on her side of
the water.

The two sides of my family are separated by water
but neither side of the Volta river is mine. I give gifts
to my relatives when I go back so the black
of my body can witness
the way I try to earn its respect. I am the only daughter
of a woman who remembers

every child she lost before me. I try to remember
them all but they exist mostly when I am on the
aeroplane, water
far below my feet. Still, I believe when I have my own
daughter
I will think of my siblings more often, and that will be a
gift.
I tell you all this for you to witness.
I am wary of placing my name next to yours, but we are
both Black

artists, both daughters using art to help remember
things forgotten. The Black of me feels it knows the Water
of you. These gifts you give enable me to witness.

Selina Nwulu

A History of Banning

after Executive Order 13769

they banned us from our countries banned us from theirs
till the earth became scorched with eviction they banned
us from our bodies left us dismembered until we were
heads bobbing on trees lungs flowered by gas injections
sliced ears flung across a field they banned us from our
labour wrung our sweat into water fountains we could not
drink from they banned us from our classrooms splintered
our minds spun gibberish out of our wisdoms banned us
from our tongues made our languages a deadweight
swinging in the back of our throats spiked our voices
heavy with grief they banned us from praise locked our
names in quarantine to wither under sun they banned us
from shops from our clothes our garments spoke a beaten
birdsong banned us from our lovers threw the light of our
laughter into fire they banned us from burial stripped us
of ritual and quest they banned us from wonder what
haven't they banned us from? what won't we take back?

Mango Tree

Mother, you are cutting that mango with a chainsaw.
Its teeth have left it with a coat of angry track marks
and yet it remains a closed fist. You bought the mango
 too soon,
ignored the insolence of its skin, thought you could soften
its bluntness and carve it a better name.

The summer we flew back to your favourite mango tree
we found it as you'd left it; fruit overladen,
branches benevolent. I ran to your stride
as you retraced your footsteps back
to the ribcage of the tree. You shook its girth

until the most fickle of mangoes lost their will,
golden grenades surrounded our feet.
You sliced the best one with a skilled deftness,
mango juice down your fingers, you laughed
as my eyes willed to taste. *That laugh*

as if fallen from the tree, luscious and oozing through
blushed skin, full of fat pulp, glistening under sun,
sweet on my lips. We sat under the mango tree
and you spoke to me in Igbo and mango. Its strings
 lodged
between my teeth for the rest of the day.

Back here you are a sculptor trying to sigh life
into this cold boulder. It stays prude and indifferent
to the sharpness of the blade. I watch its anaemic curls
wizen into northern air, see how it leaves
bitter secrets in the hollow of your mouth.

I miss your laugh.

When the Party Is Over

In memory of Belly Mujinga, Christopher Kapessa, Shukri Abdi and many more

Blackface

another terror, distorted
reflection in a fairground mirror.

For some savage play, the costume afro,
smeared mud ritual and growl;
revelling in their rage, the spectacle
of wickedness absorbed by blackness.

For others the finger wag and tongue pop,
edges and box braids, melanin in makeup,
contoured and juicy, twerk of the party
shows me I'm telling my story all wrong.

I watch them run away with our effigies,
knowing it is only a matter of time
before someone spits venom in one of our faces
or a child is found face down in a riverbed.

Everyone else disappears when the party is over,
our bodies trampled on and tossed back to us.

Gboyega Odubanjo

Dip

pastor wet me down. please today undo me.
when i was younger i got pulled bawling from the tub.
i would soak till i was pruned and let the
  lukewarm stew me.
only a matter of time before the lights went out and
  while the generator started up i'd look upon a dark
  blue me.
all this time it felt like i'd been swimming in a drum till
  the lid came off and i was borned a new me.
and it was on this day that it was said that this world
  belongs to me.
and i dare any man come here and try slew me.
promise me that when i'm gone
  you won't let anyone try say they knew me.
the only place of rest for me will be where i was made
  and came to know myself so please on that day
  subsume me.

Arrangements

i heard barely anyone turned up for the last one. those
who did only brought flowers. as if chrysanthemums
will impress anyone
in that gated suburb of clouds they call heaven.
no thank you.
i would rather die young and have a horse slaughtered
in celebration than wither without even the blood
of a chicken sprayed in my name.
and please. make sure all of my wives are seated together.
everyone must grieve.
if you see any children that you don't recognise
accompanied by women sit them at the front.
the tailor will already have everybody's fabrics and
measurements well in advance.
i will need the grief to be drawn out so when everyone
has arrived
bolt the doors. ration the food and drink. pay the band at
the end of each day.
pay the choir for the week.
give the people more time than they need
so that everyone can give eulogy and on the fourth
or fifth day once they begin to bargain in their grief and
they beg you to let them leave that is when you bring
in the palm wine. straight from the sap. now look
at how they gulp and go stupid with their grief. listen to
their cries. tell them i cannot hear them. that it isn't
loud enough.

Man

after Nicole Sealey

no manners always manic in the manor where manaman
demand dismantling mandatory unmanning
there's too many man too many many –
remand the policeman lawman informants
got the hangman on pager
understand that it's us man and it's them man
and when i say us man i proper mean all of us
man's adamant about semantics bildungsroman not a
romance
go mano a mano with the badman
the mannish winner takes mansion and manilla
but if man know you then it's just mandem innit
come nyam manna at the mangrove we the menace and
the manager singing mantra till the morning come
in the name of my man somebody say amen

Louisa Adjoa Parker

There are moments I forget

like the dark canopy of trees
lining the road from Uplyme,
the grey pebbles on the beach,
the hills we climbed
pushing our babies in buggies,

the silver light over Lyme Bay,
the plump white moon that looked
as though it would fall into the sea;
the wine-red carpet, musty velvet
curtains in the drawing room at Rosehill;

the grapes rotting on the vine outside.

You are at the root of me. It's hard
to say *this happened on that day*,
or *that happened the next,* because
you are part of everything, there
or not there; it seems as though

we only spoke last week.
Your voice, there,
as it has always been,
saying my name
like a song.

You're

You're in the blues and carmine-reds
and golds of the paint you brushed
onto canvases, in the word *Love*
written in the corner of a canvas
washed in pink.
You're in the sunlight pooling
on the floor, elongating shadows
of the mourners' legs.
You're suspended
in the glittering dust, in the notes
of our voices as we sing.
You're in your daughter's laugh,
at the edges of her smile. In your brother's lips,
your nephew's black hair, in the petals
of the white orchids fallen on the table.

Housewarming

August. Nights are drawing in.
Two decades on, your daughter
has returned to the patch of land
she came from. We're in her garden:
long stretch of lawn, next door's
one-eyed dog ambles over grass,
Flower lights hang from the washing line.
Your hammock strung on wooden posts.
In the distance, yellow fields, a vast,
pale sky. Her grandmother's farm.
Wasps hover too close to us, giddy
with the scent of beer. A burning log
sends sprays of orange sparks into night air.
Bats fly overhead. Howard plays
dancehall, funk, head bent, decks
swapped for a laptop. His beard
is white, the children grown now,
but it's as though time
has stood still and I'll turn and see you
next to me. Instead, I'm dancing
with our grown-up daughters
under a scattering of stars.

Roger Robinson

Gold

A black man with dreads and stonewash jeans is palming stuff into the hands of frail people who are walking up to him in Brixton. The police turn the corner and jump out the car and he puts what's in his hands quickly into his mouth. They ask him to open his mouth, he opens his mouth and all his teeth are gold. The sun reflecting on the gold teeth is drawing attention. People start to film on their mobile phones. The police become aware of the gathering crowd. They ask him what he's doing? He says he's giving gold to poor people. They ask him to check his pockets. He tells them to go ahead. They start pulling out handfuls of gold nuggets so pure they're nearly yellow. They ask him where did he get all this gold from? He says he's the great, great, great grandchild of Mansa Mussa, the richest African that ever lived. They ask him his name, he says George Mansa Mussa. They run a check on his name, he has no prior record. They arrest him anyway. He asks them why he's being arrested. They say he needs a permit to deal with gold. He says he's not a dealer, he's giving it away for free. They arrest him, anyway, put cuffs on him and press his head down into the car. By the time they turn the corner the chain links of the handcuffs are turning gold.

Aba Shanti Soundsystem

Aba Shanti Soundsystem could shake the trauma out of you with pure bass sound. Black people had already known this. In order to combat hundreds of years of trauma they had become accustomed to particular frequencies of bass and certain rhythms of drums to relieve all their generational hurt. Certain rhythms became very valued by black people. These healing frequencies became wailing blues and Jazz in America became whispering Samba in Brasil, became soca in Trinidad and became and became and became. Now Aba Shanti he had every principal healing frequency on 45 vinyl. It is said that he lives in a big house but sleeps only in one room as every other room held black 45 vinyl including the bathroom. As with anything else soon white people heard of the healing and felt like they had to get some even though they were not sure of the illness that they were suffering but they knew that something was not right, but the frequencies spoke differently to them. It made them dance, but it was a dance that made them grieve the transgressions of their generations. Made them cry hysterically with a deep deep sorrow and drop out from the system and twist their blond flowing hair into dreadlocks. Healing still, but healing different ills.

Denise Saul

The Room Between Us

There you are, beside the telephone stand,
waiting for me in a darkened room
when I force open the white door.
There you lie, behind it.

I never found out why you grabbed
a pewter angel instead of the receiver
when you tried to call me that morning.
I give up trying to lift you from the floor

as the room is no longer between us.
You point again to the Bible, door, wall
before I whisper, *It's alright, alright,*
now tell me what happened before the fall.

Instructions For Yellow

Saul's diary entry for September 2014: *I feel nothing from the sunlight that falls on my face.*

It is impossible that we will talk about it again.

A person in a room is affected by the colour of the walls.

The yellowness we see in the garden is not a daffodil.

She did not want us to wear black at the wake.

I can't recall who was silent first.

And yellow will look the most vivid against a dark background.

I thought she whispered something about the room but she wanted to say –

The Viewing

Behind another brown door into a windowless room
Julie the director removes the lace veil
and maps her fingers on my mother's cheek.

Perfect skin, so smooth. No wrinkles, she says
as I walk around the room to view the off-white
dress and beret covered with cream pearls.

I want to tell my mother about how she still holds light,
and that this is the last day of seeing each other.
Julie says she spent the afternoon reading aloud

the horoscopes page from the daily newspaper.
I thank Julie for sitting with her as she always does.
No trouble at all. Virgo? she asks.

Standing by the table, I bend over my mother again
to take in the smell of Floris rose perfume.
No, Libra, I tell her. *Libra.*

Kim Squirrell

Walking Home from School

For days they prise up paving slabs
along your road, workmen stripped
to the waist – roasted skin slick with sweat.

You walk past them with a caution
reserved for unchained dogs – fold
arms across your breasts.

When they make a noise in their throats,
or say a word, you blush to your fingertips,
down your legs – anger bubbles your gut.

  Untie your hair, let it loose.
  Let it writhe and hiss – turn
  their eyes to stone.

Healing

I made space for my sick body, cast aside
cooking pots and shopping lists, laid her down
in the sunshine on the grass. I let her kneel

to weed and water, I didn't mind how slowly
she scraped the trowel through the soil
or if she lost her grip.

I sent her early to bed, left her late to rise.
When she didn't want to speak, I let her tongue
grow heavy, sent messages to her eyes.

When she wasn't hungry, I fetched her dark cherries
and sweet sad music. When she wept,
I opened the floodgates, lifted her head above the tide.

I allowed no word of self-reproach,
banished *if* and *but* from her vocabulary,
polished *when* and *will* until they shone,

until they glowed in the dark. And when
she came back to me, unsure of her new form,
smaller, worn, scarred, I held her hand.

I Want to Write a Poem About Togetherness

I go up to my room, the scratch of my pen
the only company I crave.

From the kitchen my son on the piano,
a kettle rises to the boil. My husband closes a door.

Lying in bed this morning
I stroked the back of his hand,

where days of sunshine bloom
in brown rosettes of pigment:

hours spent hauling sail,
pruning orchards, digging.

Last night we Zoomed my family,
I played an old video of us at Mum's,

just the sisters
and their children.

The one who comes late,
the one who leaves early,

the one who brings the food
and me, behind the camera.

This is as far as I get
before my son comes upstairs:

'Do you know that Tokyo,
in Japanese, has only two syllables

but we make it three?
'Tow-ki-yo.'

He wraps his whole body around me,
fits his head into the curve of my neck,

smothers me in his warm breath.
'Hug me,' he says.

Warsan Shire

Backwards

The poem can start with him walking backwards into a room.
He takes off his jacket and sits down for the rest of his life,
that's how we bring Dad back.
I can make the blood run back up my nose, ants rushing into a hole.
We grow into smaller bodies, my breasts disappear,
your cheeks soften, teeth sink back into gums.
I can make us loved, just say the word.
Give them stumps for hands if even once they touched us without consent,
I can write the poem and make it disappear.
Stepdad spits liquor back into glass,
Mum's body rolls back up the stairs, the bone pops back into place,
maybe she keeps the baby.
Maybe we're okay kid?
I'll rewrite this whole life and this time there'll be so much love,
you won't be able to see beyond it.

You won't be able to see beyond it,
I'll rewrite this whole life and this time there'll be so much love.
Maybe we're okay, kid,
maybe she keeps the baby.
Mum's body rolls back up the stairs, the bone pops back into place,
Stepdad spits liquor back into glass.
I can write the poem and make it disappear,
give them stumps for hands if even once they touched us without consent,

I can make us loved, just say the word.
Your cheeks soften, teeth sink back into gums
we grow into smaller bodies, my breasts disappear.
I can make the blood run back up my nose, ants rushing into a hole,
that's how we bring Dad back.
He takes off his jacket and sits down for the rest of his life.
The poem can start with him walking backwards into a room.

Midnight in the Foreign Food Aisle

Dear Uncle, is everything you love foreign
or are you foreign to everything you love?
We're all animals and the body wants what
it wants, trust me, I know. The blonde said
Come in, love, take off your coat, what do
you want to drink?

Love is not haram but after years of fucking
women who are unable to pronounce your name,
you find yourself totally alone, in the foreign
food aisle, beside the turmeric and saffron,
remembering you mother's warm, dark hands,
prostrating in front of the halal meat, praying in a
language you haven't used in years.

Rommi Smith

from Palette for a Portrait of Little Richard

My pictures are a response to the music – they're not really portraits [. . .] the main point of the picture is the feeling that one gets from it emotionally [. . .]"
– Dave Oxtoby, painter and portraitist
of Little Richard.

Little Richard, King of the Blues . . .
and the Queen, too!
– Little Richard

I. Pitch
the wish in a sharecropper's holler
sung across midnight.

II. Tubman's[1] Moon
searchlight for a key
in the form of a treble clef.

1. Harriet Tubman, leader and strategist of the Underground Railroad, the network of safehouses and escape routes for runaway enslaved Africans.

III. Joy
the colour of the sun
the dawn Du Bois'[2] *Souls* were born.

VI. 'Sissy-Boy!'
haunts Little Richard Penniman
all the way down Pleasant Hill
past the 'Coloreds Only Waiting Room'.
He's on the next train out
of Georgia's Macon Station
and he'll never quite return –
though *Lucille* may will him home again.

XI. Revelations
Evangelist of fine-tuned, feather-tailed flamboyance.
Gospeller of bare-chested, hotpant-hipped hoodoo.
Preacher of the inner thigh
of the groove
your mama made you to.

---

2. W.E.B. Du Bois, Africanist, eminent scholar of Black American experience and co-founder of the National Association for the Advancement of Colored People (NAACP). The Souls of Black Folk (1903) is his seminal book of critical essays reflecting on race and racism and examining Black protest. The book intertwines critical and cultural philosophical thinking with references including spirituals, hymns and songs. The second chapter is entitled: 'Of the Dawn of Freedom'.

'Premonitioner' of Prince,
Sing[ing] [his] Body Electric:
joy as spark and vein as current;
ignition to the engine of the red Corvette.

A paintbrush's arc of orange, amber, ochre
can only hope to capture
the clues between War Hawk's[3] holler
in thirties Macon, Georgia
and a burning Minnesota skyline
filled with risk,
as it's expressed –
through fire.

3. Little Richard's childhood nickname.

Yomi Ṣode

On Fatherhood: Proximity to Death

Without hope, without fear – Caravaggio

Cuz, Summer 2015, knuckles clipped my chin before I could
think. I can't recall feeling like a father or a partner at that point.
I swung blindly, feeling the pain of bone hitting teeth,
translating *Give me the keys!* As *Run.*

Pieces of fabric on the pavement. This abruptness,
like a jerked needle stunned across vinyl.
When that fear hits, when death looks you in the face . . . ?
How timely of God to remind me I'll lose.

Aged ten, it was a car on Old Kent Road when I forgot
to look right. I levitated for three seconds, counting each spin
before the thud of concrete snapped me back to blaring horns:
Are you ok? Thirteen: after having a few phones of mine
jacked by olders in and out of the manor, my street smarts
soon began to calculate the seconds I had to answer

What ends you man from?   or
                                                  Bro, what size foot are you?
knowing each second it took to give my answer
would change the outcome. (You know dem ones?)

Fourteen. I watched a man park up outside my school,
open his boot then walk towards Simon, the mandem and me.
Baseball bat in hand outside of Chaucer. He wanted a body.
It wasn't going to be ours, not that day – so we ran.

19, 21, 27, 34, whatever,
when my eye catches another man's eye on road,
our intimate proximity is timed at three seconds, max.
Four seconds in, we decide the way forward. *Manorism*:
whether one yields to the other and keeps walking,
or whether we both head-nod to mark a familiarity as skin folk.

Five seconds in, should none of the above occur,
the proximity will break.

It was a snowy day in Brixton when I saw the kid
riding by on a bike, then U-turning through the slush
shouting, *What, bruv?* to the side of me.
My music already on pause from when our eyes met,
pre-empting the battle cry.

What, bruv! Fist clenched,
What bruv! waiting.

My legs rushed into oncoming traffic. I did not want to leave
but I walked away like some dickhead, like I was scared
but I wasn't. I was vex. I'm a big man, hands up apologising
to each car stopping to let me pass. Feeling less man, less brave.

Most nights, my son whispers *I love you*
then rests his head on my chest,
long enough to birth a new fear of death.
Thirty-six. Is this how it works?
The estimation of risk, the feeling of a tired squeeze.
And all I have to lose right there, looking up at me.

[Insert Name]'s Mother: A Ghazal

Sing me something. A sun rising above a tower block, a song.
On mornings, watching him stretch before my eyes, a magical song.

Day seven, my body now numb has turned its back on me.
If this is mourning, I want his spirit here to sing us a farewell song.

Pastor, how does thou forgive? Each exhale stains this house,
I am sinning in my grief. Congregation, bless me a song.

So much food untouched that will rot. Nothing is staying.
My boy on the news, smiling on his graduation day, we sang a song.

Earlier years, each step was like water crashing against rocks.
We watched him grow, two stepping the ghouls away in song.

Hold me. Stay as if it were summer where love was our biggest risk.
Lover, permit me a night to be willing. To arc my back in a song.

Policeman. Though I speak, I cannot hear myself. *He was never in a gang!*
Listen to me please, you stubborn song.

The fridge hums sadness, the light is faulty. Silence is unbearable.
House, perhaps there is a meaning hidden somewhere, a song.

No, he didn't leave you because you finished the jam, no, listen. Baby boy,
lightning struck and up shot a beanstalk to the heavens! A distracting song.

The spirit never dies. And every day I search. I can't feel him.
Can he hear me, Yomi? Crying, praying, singing a song.

On Fatherhood: Envy

My son *oooohs* at an advert, declaring his right to roam
the MIDDLE AT LIDL section, never mind
the Waitrose, Asda or Tesco I suggested we visit instead.

I remember pulling my hood up when walking out of Lidl.
The ridicule man would receive in school if I got caught.
The triggers in seeing it celebrated now.

When asked what superhero he wants to be for World Book Day,
my son says *Miles Morales*. I ask him why. He says, *Because he looks like me, Dad. Maybe a spider can bite me, and I can fly, like he does.*

My son tethers his tablet to the TV, rapping along to Stormzy,
I am young, Black, beautiful and brave. He asks who Malorie Blackman is;
he asks whether Stormzy is a poet, like me.

I spot a child on a busy road, riding past me on her bike,
her father supervising behind. My aneephya is quick to dismiss
the thought of my son and me doing the same. I question why.

I envy my son. I watch him, an air bender, so daring.
Shaping himself to the wind's current. *Is this not my purpose?*
I ask myself. *Watching my own live a life I couldn't.*

Aneephya / ʌh,ni:fɪə /

Aneephyitis is the release of the aneephya toxin into the blood stream. Announced by a sound similar to that of knuckles quietly cracking, it is triggered roughly between ages 9–11, continuing into adulthood, and later old age. This is specific to Black people as a result of weathering and trauma carried down generations.

Aneephya: In relation to ancestry.

Degna Stone

over **(→)** *prep. adv.*

after A. Van Jordan

1. Above or beyond: She sang along to 'Somewhere Over the Rainbow', never imagining her own shoes could be ruby slippers, could carry her away. When she was a girl, her imagination always led to trouble. She soon learned that daydreamers were fools, bit by bit she locked her dreams inside. **2. Throughout the duration of**: Over the years it became apparent that they couldn't stand the sight, the smell, the thought of each other. **3. On the opposite side of**: They could barely hold a civil conversation over the dinner table. **4. In consideration**: She goes over the list of things that piss her off about him every night as she brushes her teeth too hard. The way he talks down to her as if she's stupid, the way he hates her friends, the way he made her think she loved him, needed him and then grew distant. She spits blood into the sink. **5. In repetition**: She scrawled T.L.N.D. across her schoolbooks, carved it around the empty ink well on her desk. Did she really believe back then that true love never dies? Love is not a constant. You must fall in love over and over and over again. **6. In reference to, concerning**: *What are we fighting over?* **7. Too great, excessive**: Her mother always told her she was oversensitive. **8. Through all parts of**: She stands naked in front of the bathroom mirror looking over her body, running her hands over her skin, trying to remember what it felt like when he touched her. **9. Recovered from the effects of**: Though there was never an exact date, she marked every birthday that would have passed. *How can you celebrate the birthday of someone never born? Why aren't you over it by now?* **10. Submerge or bury**: She sank down and let the water close over her head.

Another Tongue

Missing words take flight, birdlike,
arrive in new countries, lost
amongst flocks of alien language.

Interpretation becomes a tangle
of mistranslated letters. Distorted
representations tear at our tongues.

We learn new words slowly.
Slower than our children, shielded
from our struggle.

How to Unpick the Lies?

It's the first day of the last month of the first year of this decade.
The peace we were hoping for is lost to us.
Taught from a young age that white lies are harmless,
we hold on to ideas of ourselves that have never been true.

In our family, we named the tooth fairy Esther.
Our youngest would wrap her lost tooth in a handwritten note,
Esther wrote tiny letters of wisdom in reply.

The lies we tell ourselves are exquisite, vivid in detail
that sounds so true we've learned to believe them.
Learned to walk
through the world with our dicks still hard for the illusion of power.
We have forgotten how to recognise truth.

When our youngest was seven she learned about blackness
when two men were convicted of the murder of a boy.
Learned its proximity to danger, its closeness to death.

The Monarch has no plans to change the titles she bestows
on behalf of a non-existent Empire, divorced from bloodshed and terror.
Think Merchant Ivory and empire-line dresses, not Amritsar massacre.
The Empire is the empire is the Commonwealth is a spectre.

As our youngest grew older and figured out the truth,
it broke me. I'd disguised white lies as magic
to make the world seem beautiful. Bearable.

When we talk about Nation, we keep the truth from ourselves,
hide behind *The Golden Age*, *Enlightenment*, *Industrial Revolution*. Progress.
If you don't like it, fuck off back where you come from!
But where do I come from if not here? This country. My country.

Keisha Thompson

Some Have Beaten Suffering

a found poem from *The Princess Bride* transcript

I caught your breath for ransom
what is it worth?
a funny high?
a chance?
a cloudy day?
your dearest love?

I never said that I knew you were
capable of love
but I dreamt a warning

where I come from
women at the table
sniff vials – get put out

reveal everything with pride then die
into a thousand pieces
the venom of love
poor and perfect
prisoners to needs, attempts
blubbering, surpassing beauty

bless me for destroying him before
he found my faithlessness

I pushed my wishes down a hill
after him
panicking
headed into the swamp
lost for doubt
quiet never-kisses
nonsense

I am a summer of screams
smothered adventure
singed memory
revenge marauding
surprise quirks
fighting

rich from inherited fear
I retire
lightning has succeeded our future
unusual light surrenders
captures us in despair
I swear I cannot save you
lies do not become us

The Concrete Square off Tib Street in May

or maybe it was June. it was warm. warm enough for us to be outside at 8 p.m. it was supposed to be a date and I guess it was. started in a suitably normal way. tea and cake in Mr Scruff's café. then we sat on a wall edge. elbows dodging nettles. watching a homeless man dancing. we gave him a pencil so he was happy. I don't tell my friends about this. they would only say I deserve more. I should have gone home. wasteman. anger. jokes. borrowed words. that curl up like dried lemon rind. I didn't mind it. no it wasn't cocktails at Red Door. was off-key. in the best way. a true date to remember. not numerically but like smelling sulphur for the first time in science. we never stopped speaking. until we kissed so I could taste failed suicide on breath. even then. I knew that I didn't want to be anywhere else.

In memory of Dave Osborn

Number 2020

1 kn0w y0u're n0t g01ng t0 6e71eve me 6ut
1've 6een th1nk1ng and 1've g0t 1t a77 5u55ed
the rea50n f0r a77 the 6700dc7art cha05
the rea50n f0r a77 the5e w0rldw1de 67under5
dunn0 a60ut y0u 6ut 1'm 67am1ng the num6er5

n0w 6ef0re y0u g0 ca5t1ng d0u6t
1 need y0u t0 at 7ea5t hear me 0ut
y0u can't d15agree 1f y0u d0n't kn0w what 1'm 0n a60ut
the f1r5t t1me y0u hear the truth 1t can 50und extreme
6ut th1nk 0f any pr067em and there'5 a num6er 1n 6etween

th1nk 6ack t0 5ch007, a77 the math5 y0u w0u7d f1ght
5h0ut1ng 0ut – when am 1 rea77y g01ng t0 u5e th15 1n 71fe
and that 15 what they wanted u5 t0 th1nk, r1ght?
they wanted u5 t0 fee7 71ke we c0u7dn't under5tand
1 5ee n0w that 1t wa5 a77 part 0f 0ne 61g p7an

1 ca77ed my fr1end up the 0ther day t0 5hare the new5
he 5a1d that 70ckd0wn had g0t me 50und1ng c0nfu5ed
e1ther that 0r 1 wa5 pu771ng h15 7eg 6ut 1t wa5n't a ru5e
the f1r5t t1me y0u hear the truth 1t can 50und extreme
6ut th1nk 0f any pr067em and there'5 a num6er 1n 6etween

1 5a1d everyOne 15 ta7k1ng a6Out COv1d but 1t'5 actua77y the 19
1've gOt nO prO67em w1th the g 6ut 1t'5 that 5 that'5 trOu671ng me
he 5a1d he'd heard enOugh and he'd ca77 me next week
1 5a1d yOu can catch me On 1n5tagram that'5 where 1'm gO1ng tO 71v1ng
thrOugh the med1um Of pure v1deO and pure 1mage

he 5a1d w1th a77 the cOd1ng 1'd 6e 6etter Off-gr1d
and what am 1 gO1ng tO dO a6Out my v1ta7 5tat15t1c5?
then he put the phOne dOwn

and 1 knOw yOu 7Ot are 7augh1ng nOw

6ut 5OOner Or 7ater thO5e num6er5 are gO1ng tO turn On u5
and yOu watch Out 6ecau5e next year 1t will be even wOr5e
f1fty year5 Of the G7a5tOnbury Fe5t1va7 and the UEFA Cup?
a77 Our 6e7Oved ann1ver5ar1e5 – they're nOt gO1ng tO add up!

even the 51mp7e equat1On5 are g1v1ng me 5tre55
71ke the num6er Of peOp7e whO vOted tO 5ave the NH5
nOw that 5hOu7d match the amOunt c7app1ng On a Thur5day n1ght
1 wa5 crunch1ng 6ut thO5e num6er5 ju5t were nOt cOm1ng Out r1ght

50 c7ear7y there'5 a f7aw, 1 can't dea7 w1th the5e f1gure5 anym0re
71ke ethn1c m1n0r1t1e5' chance 0f dy1ng fr0m C0v1d 15 f0ur t1me5 m0re
0r that e1ght m1nute5 + 0ne knee + 0ne neck = th1rd degree murder
15 1t any w0nder that 1 am up t0 here w1th a77 the numer1ca7 murmur?
1 d0n't want t0 6e part 0f a 5y5tem that make5 me fee7 71ke a 5tat15t1c
da17y update5 try1ng t0 c0nv1nce u5 that y0u can carry the 0ne 0n a pandem1c?
churn1ng 0ut num6er5 t0 c0ver up m155ed target5 and fa75e fact5
50 1 d15tract my5e7f 6y p05t1ng up tr1v1a7 c0mment5
t0 5ee h0w many 71ke5 1t w177 attract
that 15 the p07yrhythm1c 50und 0f hyp0cr15y
th15 c077ect1ve 1507at10n 15 hav1ng a negat1ve 1mpact 0n me
and trauma 15n't 50meth1ng y0u can 5u6tract
50 1 5ay 1t'5 t1me t0 act

1t'5 t1me f0r a num6er5 60yc0tt
6urn the ca7endar5 and 7eave the ca7cu7at0r5 t0 r0t
cut y0ur tape mea5ure, da5h away y0ur a6acu5, the wh07e 70t
ju5t 5t0p c0unt1ng
70rd kn0w5 1've 5t0pped c0unt1ng the day5
at 7ea5t 1t w177 he7p w1th c71mate change
1f y0u take the num6er5 0ut 0f the 51tuat10n5
the g706a7 temperature can't g0 up 0r d0wn

can't 6e a part 0f a rece5510n 1f there'5
n0 va7ue attached t0 my p0und
5crap the exchange rate and 1nf7at10n
a77 the emergency rate5 0f deva5tat10n
1t ju5t g0e5 away . . .

Kandace Siobhan Walker

Art Pop

Learning to drive in bare feet as a way to survive.
Blue jeans make you feel dishonest sticky
indiscreet. Stimming is just like walking the pavement
at night waiting for your favourite line
in your favourite scene. Whenever you're crying
you feel just human enough to drink rain or chew
green sugarcane in the heat like the perfume-wearing
  women
you wanna be kissing in strangers' backseats.
We're not winning any championship trophies
but it's always fascinating when you tell a new lie.
You're alive now but this used to be my playground.
Can't tell if he thinks you're talkative or just high. At the
  visa counter
trying to explain what you mean when you say it's giving
  blue.
Walk slow, head down, a face in the crowd. We feel like
  magic
when we're acting: keep dancing, keep dancing.
What could be worse than social rejection? Dare you to
ask the moon if she knows she's just a reflection.

Eye Contact

I can't antagonise the person I want to be into being.
Hierarchy means we can be friends now and
acquaintances later.
I call anything anything. This is intimacy. This Blue
Mountains, this green banana.
My body doesn't speak a language because I'm rarely ever
in my body.
This chest of trumpets is psychotherapy. We can't afford
these trumpets.
Try to be present in myself. I might discover I have too
many bedrooms.
I want to be tied down. Nights out are just weighted
blankets with conversation.
I'm not an artist, I'm a woman lagging behind realtime. I
wake up taller every day,
worrying about whether I was kinder back when I didn't
know what I don't know.

Sugar, Sugar, Honey, Honey

Apologies, I didn't text you back because I was thinking and panicking.
Stuff like, spirits can read your mind, probably. Are people whose Spotify's
set to public in need of more interiority? Why do I eat only the blue M&M's?
I daydream obsessively about falling in love and dying, and I wonder
if this is normal? I think I might be broken or worse, whole. I think
everyone can sense my secondhand lonely when I wear knee-high boots.
As a kid I believed music on the radio came from the sky. I think I'm having a
human experience, but I don't know if I should be proud or embarrassed by it.
I'm tired of talking in images so other people can understand.
I just want you guys to get it!
My brain lives captive in a windowless skeleton, a nutshell full of melon pulp, an unrecognisable pink person sitting in a pitch, starry room with a podcast mic.

Warda Yassin

Swift

I saw swifts today, a small ashy vortex
turning scarf in the maghrib sky, and I remembered
the poet in Ledbury who told me they were

African visitors here for the summer. I thought
of my grandmother, but not with her wings jammed
against the back of a floral chair in a tiny box,

instead a swift with scythelike wings curved
skywards in her burgundy jilbab, eyelashes flooded
with rain prayer, her hair soft patches of henna like

copper burning through streams. All those mid-flight
duas that will never land. Now, I watch the flight
of aunties whirling through living rooms, arguing

over this last winter, the cost of oak, never giving
the daughters-in-law her gold bangles, and how
the war turned their summers here into a lifetime.

Treetop Hotel

My weddings get started after midnight,
shedding trench coats like insecurities, revealing
black swan necks, gold-hooped wrists, all of us
a swarm of sparkle, making way for the bride
to strut down a phone-lit runway lathered in yellow
mustard beads, swathed in red, gold, green.
Rattling our tongues like it's B Town, Somaliland.
A security guard trolling screens for background booty.
Girls peacocking – *who you got on Snapchat?*
Flipping their hair back, leaving aunties dangling
in the doorway, dancefloor waxed in R&B.
That mother-daughter dance. At least one girl
mushrooming the rest, with a fro so big and heels
so skinny. The boys we'd like to love hovering
like a bad idea. The windows steamed with light
gossip, no backbite reaching Gell Street, names
frothing across lips, sipping pink cardamom,
my dress stitched to my skin, my abaaya
oceaning as I step outside to catch my breath,
the buraanbur odes of the elders chanting
our beauty, to behold, held – asli, qaali.

Miss Yassin

is a granite heart, heavy inside shoulders that recoil
at the sight of a child's sadness. In the staffroom,
she is a geographer tallying a Richter scale
of Prevent comments, like when Stacey said

Muslim boys can't write about mountains.
Those times she becomes a coastline coming for a city.
In A8 she is a mustard cardie that never dresses
for the weather, only the policies hailing down

on us all, like the silent rules of *only two*
black-brown writers allowed. She is uncertain
whether she's shiny or pallid, or a midi dress
with flying foxes for hands. Maybe she is

a child's gift of an emerald cartoon, talking eyebrows
and half-mooned eyes. Or perhaps, a lopsided turban
pulled from a drawer on the days she comes alive
at her desk, despite knowing absolutely nothing.

Belinda Zhawi

Tchaikovsky's January

The tenacity of opening my eyes
at the start of each day
in this body of creaking joints,
tight jaw and knit brow
is a cold walk along a polluted river
is a snow-capped horizon
is an insistence on living
is a romance with new beginnings bang in the middle of
the season
I was curious about my past so she came in a dream
to make sure I stay in the locked room at the back of my
head
Deep in the distant night metal grinds against concrete,
the leaves brown, death still hovers
and the workmen are in orange – hours away from the
sun
Can you hear me?
A telepathic question from the doomed
observatory blinking me coded messages in the distance:
Bring yourself, bring your self, bring yourself
Deep in the distant night metal grinds against concrete,
the leaves fall
death still hovers

and the workmen are hours away from the sun
Bring yourself, bring your self, bring yourself,
Bring yourself, bring your self, bring yourself

Runyengetero

Praise be to all that is tender; early morning prayer!
Waking from mares; eyes still closed in relieved prayer

In praise of falling into the day, cracking of joints
& the most high for this qaafiya, this refrain, this prayer

Praise be to that old cliché of feeling small next to a
body of water headed elsewhere. Is that not prayer?

Praise be the horizon, how it can go on & on
& on just like my mother's daily five a.m. prayer

for her children's right to leave their home
& make it back alive – to avoid prayer

under a last breath. The water in my eyes in praise of all
that is tender. My prayer

is to see how far I can stretch on nothing but prayer

& the water in my eyes. Salty memories left in the sea,
the sand – a prayer

prayed with no regard for the answer
Give us the right words so the prayer

rings exactly how it should because grace is precise
Favour wields a straight arrow & mercy comes from
prayer

This Body Wants What It Wants

There are ghosts in this body   ghosts on the night bus,
ghosts in the mind, ghosts on the morning train & in
the house plants.
This body is the railtracks that mar the solace of dawn,
this body is nothing like a moment of pause, a pocket of
calm. This body is the tidal creek out back
whose mouth is a confluence of two rivers
This body is reminded of when it boarded the train that
used to
go both ways –
that is now just a one-way trip.
This body is a full half of the day; empty the
rest.
Empty the boats still sitting on the naked creek bed when
the water is low.
This body wants sun. It wants a
large mirror   on the floor, to sit in front of   legs
open hands   eyes   curious. That's what grownups
do
After a month-long food and lovers fast this body still
struggles to hear its God so it's plotting its way back
to where it began, in search of some negative space; a
moment of pause   with nothing but the memory of
water
crawling from its eyes to the bone in the jaw. The salt of
the sea is the same as that of the water in these eyes
–

This body wants to play play this body wants to play this
body this body this body wants sun. this body is real this

body lives breeds this body is strong this body is typed this body is soft this body is smart this body is this body makes sounds this body holds me this body keeps me this body helps me to understand my experience on this earth this body is the only thing I own the only thing I came with and I will go back with this body this this body this this this body this body is black this body is brown this body is pink in some bits this body is deep this body was not made for work this body was made to shirk so don't let me go berserk this body laughs they want to play this body, they want to play this body, they want to play this body, and then they want to play. The body, a real entity that lives, breeds, is strong, is typed, is gentle, is smart, growls, holds me, helps me to understand my existence on earth, is the only thing I own, the only thing I came with, and I will go back with this body, this body, this body, this body, this body, this body, this body, the body, the body, the body, the body, the body, the body, the body, the body, the body, the body, the body, the body, the body, the body

Contributors

Jason Allen-Paisant is from a village called Coffee Grove in Manchester, Jamaica. He is a Lecturer in Caribbean Poetry and Decolonial Thought in the School of English at the University of Leeds, where he is also the Director of the Institute for Colonial and Postcolonial Studies. He serves on the editorial board of *Callaloo: A Journal of African Diaspora Arts and Letters* and holds a doctorate in Medieval and Modern Languages from the University of Oxford. He lives in Leeds with his partner and two daughters. His first poetry collection, *Thinking with Trees*, was named a 2021 *Irish Times* Poetry Book of the Year and was highly commended in the Forward Prizes.

Raymond Antrobus MBE, FRSL was born in Hackney, London, to an English mother and Jamaican father. He is the author of *Shapes & Disfigurements* (Burning Eye, 2012), *To Sweeten Bitter* (Out-Spoken Press, 2017), *The Perseverance* (Penned in the Margins/Tin House, 2018) and *All The Names Given* (Picador/Tin House, 2021).

Dean Atta was named as one of the most influential LGBT people in the UK by the *Independent on Sunday*. His debut poetry collection, *I Am Nobody's Nigger*, was shortlisted for the Polari First Book Prize. His young-adult novel in verse, *The Black Flamingo*, won the 2020 Stonewall Book Award, and was shortlisted for the CILIP Carnegie Medal, the YA Book Prize and the Jhalak Prize.

Janette Ayachi is a Scottish-Algerian poet. She is the author of two pamphlets, *Pauses at Zebra Crossings* and *A Choir of Ghosts*, plus a hardback children's book, *The Mermaid, the Girl and the Gondola* (Black Wolf, 2016), illustrated by Fabio Perla. Her first full-length poetry collection *Hand Over Mouth Music* (Pavilion: University of Liverpool Press, 2019) won the Saltire Poetry Book of the Year 2019. She is writing her next poetry book *QuickFire, Slow Burning* (Pavilion, 2023), and *Lonerlust*, a memoir about travelling alone searching landscapes, culture, desire and human connection.

Dzifa Benson is a Ghanaian-British multi-disciplinary artist whose work intersects science, art, language, the body and ritual, which she explores through poetry, theatre-making, performance, curation, essays and criticism. She abridged and adapted the National Youth Theatre REP Company's 2021 production of *Othello* in collaboration with Olivier Award-winning director Miranda Cromwell. Dzifa is a Ledbury Poetry Critic whose byline, covering theatre, poetry, fiction and non-fiction, appears in the *Telegraph*, *Financial Times* and the *Times Literary Supplement*. She is a Jerwood Compton Poetry Fellow 2021/2022 and Poet-in-Residence curator for Whitstable Biennale 2022.

Malika Booker is a British poet of Guyanese and Grenadian parentage and the founder of Malika's Poetry Kitchen. Her collection *Pepper Seed* (Peepal Tree Press, 2013) was shortlisted for the OCM Bocas Poetry Prize 2014 and the Seamus Heaney Centre Prize. She received her MA from Goldsmiths University, was Cultural Fellow in Creative Writing at Leeds University, and is now a Lecturer at MMU. Malika was the first British poet to become a fellow of Cave Canem, was the inaugural Poet-in-Residence at the Royal Shakespeare Company, and has represented British writing internationally, both independently and with the British Council.

Eric Ngalle Charles is a Cameroon-born, Wales-based writer, poet, playwright, actor and activist. He holds an MA in Creative Writing from Swansea University. His autobiography, *I, Eric Ngalle*, was published by Parthian Books. Eric was selected by Jackie Kay as one of the UK's top ten BAME writers.

Inua Ellams FRSL is an internationally touring poet, playwright, performer, graphic artist and designer. He is an ambassador for the Ministry of Stories and his published books of poetry include *Candy Coated Unicorns and Converse All Stars*, *Thirteen Fairy Negro Tales*, *The Wire-Headed Heathen*, *#Afterhours* and *The Half-God of Rainfall* – an epic story in verse. His first play *The 14th Tale* was awarded a Fringe First at the Edinburgh International Theatre Festival and his fourth *Barber Shop Chronicles* sold out two runs at England's National Theatre. He recently completed his first full poetry collection, *The Actual*, is currently touring *An Evening with An Immigrant* and working on several commissions across stage and screen. In graphic art and design, online and in print, he tries to mix the old with the new, juxtaposing texture and pigment with flat colour and vector graphics. He lives and works from London, where he founded the Midnight Run, a nocturnal urban excursion.

Samatar Elmi is a poet, PhD candidate and educator. He is an Obsidian Fellow, was shortlisted for the Venture Award and is a graduate of the Young Inscribe Mentoring Programme. Poems have appeared widely, including in *Poetry Review*, *Magma* and *Iota*. Elmi's *Portrait of Colossus* (flipped eye, 2021) was selected as the Poetry Book Society (PBS) Summer 2021 Pamphlet Choice.

Khadijah Ibrahiim is a poet of Jamaican parentage, born in the city of Leeds. She is the Artistic Director of Leeds Young Authors and the Producer of Leeds Youth Poetry Slam Festival. Peepal Tree Press published her poetry collection *Rootz Runnin* in 2008, the same year she toured the USA with the F-words Creative Freedom Writers. As a delegate for Arts Council England (Yorkshire) she attended Calabash International Literature Festival in Jamaica and was one of the first international writers to attend the El Gouna Writers' Residency in Egypt, 2010. Hailed as one of Yorkshire's 'most prolific' poets by BBC Radio, she continues to make various stage appearances across Britain, the USA, the Caribbean and Africa. Peepal Tree Press also published her latest collection of poems, *Another Crossing*.

Keith Jarrett is a writer, performer and academic of Jamaican heritage. A multiple poetry slam champion, he was selected for the International Literary Showcase as one of ten outstanding LGBT UK-based writers. *Selah*, his debut poetry collection, was published in 2017. His poem 'From the Log Book' was projected onto the façade of St. Paul's Cathedral and broadcast as a commemorative art installation. His play *Safest Spot in Town* was performed at the Old Vic and aired on BBC Four. Keith teaches at New York University London and is completing his debut novel.

Anthony Joseph is an award-winning Trinidad-born poet, novelist, academic and musician. He is the author of four poetry collections and three novels. His 2018 novel *Kitch* was shortlisted for the Republic of Consciousness Prize, the Royal Society of Literature's Encore Award, and longlisted for the OCM Bocas Prize for Caribbean Literature. His most recent publication is the experimental novel *The Frequency of Magic*. In 2019, he was awarded a Jerwood Compton Poetry Fellowship. His new collection *Sonnets for Albert* is forthcoming from Bloomsbury in 2022. As a musician, he has released eight critically acclaimed albums, and in 2020 received a Paul Hamlyn Foundation Composers Award. He holds a PhD in Creative Writing from Goldsmiths University and is a Senior Lecturer in Creative Writing at De Montfort University.

Safiya Kamaria Kinshasa is a British-born Barbadian-raised poet and dancer whose work chiefly encompasses both disciplines. Safiya was a participant of the Jerwood Arts | Apples & Snakes Poetry in Performance Programme. Her work is published in a range of journals and anthologies including *The Caribbean Writer*, *The Amistad* and *Alter Egos* (Bad Betty

Press, 2019), *Poetry Birmingham Literary Journal* and more. She was shortlisted for the 2020 Out-Spoken Page Poetry Prize and longlisted for the Performance and Film Categories.

In 2019 she won the BBC Edinburgh Fringe Slam Championships, the UK Nationals and became a BBC Words First finalist. She has been commissioned by notable figures and organisations including The Original Wailers and BBC Bitesize.

Vanessa Kisuule is a writer and performer based in Bristol. She has won over ten slam titles including the Roundhouse Slam 2014, Hammer and Tongue National Slam 2014 and the Nuyorican Poetry Slam. She has been featured on BBC iPlayer, Radio 1 and Radio 4's *Woman's Hour*, *Blue Peter* and TEDx in Vienna. She has been invited to perform nationally and internationally, from Belgium to Brazil to Bangladesh. Her poem on the historic toppling of Edward Colston's statue, 'Hollow', went viral in the summer of 2020. She has two poetry collections published by Burning Eye Books and her work was highly commended in the 2019 Forward Poetry Prize Anthology. She was the Bristol City Poet for 2018–2020 and is currently working on her debut novel.

Rachel Long is the author of *My Darling from the Lions*, first published by Picador in 2020, and by Tin House in 2021 (US).

Adam Lowe is the LGBT+ History Month Poet Laureate and was Yorkshire's Olympic Poet for 2012. He is from Leeds but currently lives in Salford. Adam is a Fellow of the Complete Works and the Obsidian Foundation.

Nick Makoha is founder of the Obsidian Foundation and winner of the 2021 Ivan Juritz prize and the Poetry London Prize. In 2017, Nick was shortlisted for the Forward Prize for his debut *Kingdom of Gravity*. He is a Cave Canem Graduate Fellow, Malika's Kitchen Fellow and Complete Works alumnus. He won the 2015 Brunel International African Poetry Prize and the 2016 Toi Derricotte & Cornelius Eady Prize for his pamphlet *Resurrection Man*. His poems have appeared in the *Cambridge Review*, the *New York Times*, *Poetry Review*, *Rialto*, *Poetry London*, *TriQuarterly Review*, *5 Dials*, *Boston Review*, *Callaloo* and *Wasaari* among others.

Karen McCarthy Woolf's first poetry collection *An Aviary of Small Birds* was nominated for the Forward Prize for Best First Collection and Jerwood Prize, and her latest, *Seasonal Disturbances*, was a winner in the inaugural Laurel Prize. In 2019 she moved to Los Angeles as a Fulbright postdoctoral scholar and Writer-in-Residence at the Promise Institute for Human Rights at UCLA, exploring the relationship between poetry and law. 2021 took her to Brazil, as an artist-in-residence at the Sacatar Institute in Bahia, writing new work exploring sugar and its cultural and material legacies.

Momtaza Mehri is a poet, essayist and independent researcher. Her latest pamphlet, *Doing the Most with the Least*, was published by Goldsmiths Press.

Bridget Minamore is a British-Ghanaian writer from south-east London. *Titanic* (Out-Spoken Press), her debut pamphlet of poems, was published in 2016. Bridget currently works as the Writing Assistant to writer and director Alfonso Cuarón, and is working on her first novel.

Selina Nwulu is a poet and essayist, whose work focuses on social and climate justice. Her poetry and essays have been widely featured in a variety of journals, short films and anthologies, including the critically acclaimed anthology *New Daughters of Africa*. Her work has been translated into Spanish, Greek and Polish, exhibited on the Warsaw metro, in New York and Dublin. She is a former Young People's Laureate for London, was shortlisted for the Brunel International African Poetry Prize 2019, and is a 2021 Arts Award Finalist for Environmental Writing. Her debut pamphlet is entitled *The Secrets I Let Slip* (Burning Eye Books, 2015) and her first full-length collection, *A Little Resurrection*, is forthcoming with Bloomsbury in Autumn 2022.

Gboyega Odubanjo was born and raised in East London. He is an editor of *bath magg* and his debut pamphlet, *While I Yet Live*, was published by Bad Betty Press in 2019. His second pamphlet, *Aunty Uncle Poems*, published by Smith Doorstop in 2021, was a winner of the Eric Gregory Award and the Michael Marks Award.

Louisa Adjoa Parker is a British writer and poet of Ghanaian and English heritage who lives in south-west England. Her first poetry collection, *Salt-sweat and Tears*, and pamphlet *Blinking in the Light* were published by Cinnamon Press, and her third collection, *How to Wear a Skin*, was published by Indigo Dreams in 2019. Her debut short story collection, *Stay with Me*, was published in 2020 by Colenso

Books. Her latest poetry pamphlet, *She Can Still Sing*, was published in 2021 by flipped eye.

Roger Robinson is a British writer, musician and performer who lives between England and Trinidad. His book *A Portable Paradise* (Peepal Tree Press) won the T. S. Eliot Prize in 2019. He is the second writer of Caribbean heritage to win the prize, the highest value award in UK poetry, after Derek Walcott who won the 2010 prize. Robinson's victory was also seen as an important one for small presses. *A Portable Paradise* was only the second book of poetry to win the Ondaatje Prize in 2020.

Denise Saul is the author of two pamphlets. *White Narcissi* (flipped eye, 2007) was a Poetry Book Society Pamphlet Choice and *House of Blue* (Rack Press, 2012) was a PBS Pamphlet Recommen-dation. She is the recipient of the Poetry Society's Geoffrey Dearmer Prize. Her first full-length collection, *The Room Between Us*, will be published in 2022 by Pavilion Poetry, an imprint of Liverpool University Press.

Kim Squirrell was born in Birmingham to an Irish mother and Kittitian father. She is a visual artist and writer of poetry and fiction. She lives in Dorset and has worked in Environmental Theatre, Land-based Learning and Community Arts projects. Her work has appeared in *Poetry Review*, *Riptide*, *Stand*, the *Out of Bounds* poetry anthology (Bloodaxe, 2012) and the short story anthology *Resist* (Comma Press, 2019). In 2018 she was shortlisted for the Dinesh Allirajah short story prize and gained a Creative Writing MA at the University of Exeter. Kim was shortlisted for the inaugural

James Berry Poetry Prize in 2021 and won the Bridport Prize Dorset Award for her novel in progress.

Warsan Shire grew up in London. She is the author of the collections *Teaching My Mother How to Give Birth* (flipped eye, 2011), *Her Blue Body* (flipped eye, 2015), and *Our Men Do Not Belong to Us* (Slapering Hol Press and Poetry Foundation, 2015). Her poems have appeared in journals and magazines including *Poetry Review*, *Wasafiri* and *Sable LitMag*; in the anthologies *Salt Book of Younger Poets* (2011), *Long Journeys: African Migrants on the Road* (Brill, 2013), and *Poems That Make Grown Women Cry* (Simon and Schuster, 2016); as well as in Beyoncé's visual album *Lemonade* (2016). In 2013, she won Brunel University's first African Poetry Prize. In 2014, she was named the first Young Poet Laureate for London and chosen as Poet-in-Residence for Queensland, Australia. *Bless the Daughter Raised By A Voice in Her Head*, her first full-length collection, is published in 2022 by Chatto & Windus in collaboration with flipped eye.

Rommi Smith is an award-winning poet, theatre-maker and scholar. Three-time BBC Writer-in-Residence, she is the inaugural British Parliamentary Writer-in-Residence and the inaugural twenty-first-century Poet-in-Residence for Keats' House, Hampstead. A Cave Canem and Hedgebrook Fellow (USA), Rommi is winner of the Northern Writers' Prize for Poetry (selected by poet Don Paterson). This year, she is a Poet-in-Residence for the Wordsworth Trust. Rommi holds a doctorate in the study of Blues and Jazz women performers.

Yomi Ṣode is an award-winning Nigerian British writer. He is a recipient of the 2019 Jerwood Compton Poetry Fellowship and was shortlisted for The Brunel International African Poetry Prize 2021. His acclaimed one-man show *COAT* toured nationally to sold-out audiences, including at the Brighton Festival, Roundhouse Camden and the Battersea Arts Centre. In 2020 his libretto *Remnants*, written in collaboration with award-winning composer James B. Wilson and performed with Chineke! Orchestra premiered on BBC Radio Three. In 2021, his play, *and breathe . . .* premiered at the Almeida Theatre to rave reviews. Yomi is a Complete Works alumnus and a member of Malika's Poetry Kitchen. He is founder of BoxedIn, First Five, The Daddy Diaries, and mentorship programme 12 in 12. His debut collection *Manorism* will be published by Penguin Press in 2022.

Degna Stone is a contributing editor at *The Rialto*, a co-founder of *Butcher's Dog* poetry magazine, and an associate artist with The Poetry Exchange. She holds an MA in Creative Writing from Newcastle University and received a Northern Writers' Award for her poetry in 2015. She is a fellow of Inscribe (Peepal Tree Press), The Complete Works III and Obsidian Foundation. Her debut collection *Proof of Life on Earth* is forthcoming from Nine Arches Press.

Keisha Thompson is a Manchester-based writer, performance artist and producer. Keisha is Senior Learning Programme Manager for The World Reimagined, chair of radical arts funding body Future's Venture Foundation, a MOBO x London Theatre Consortium Fellow and a member of Greater Manchester Cultural and Heritage Group, and recipient of the Arts Foundation Theatre Makers Award 2021. She is currently working with commissioners Eclipse Theatre, York Theatre Royal and Pilot Theatre to stage a new play, *The Bell Curves*. The script was made in development with Box of Tricks. She is also working with Fuel Theatre and Alan Lane (Slung Low) to create a new children's show, *Izzy, BOSSS & Fractal*. In August 2020, she released a new mini album, *Ephemera*, in collaboration with Tom 'Werkha' Leah and featuring the cellist Abel Selaocoe. In 2020, she finished touring her award-winning solo show, *Man on the Moon*. Her debut book, *Lunar*, features her poetry and the show script, whilst *Moonwhile* is a poetic mini-album featuring music from the show.

Kandace Siobhan Walker is a Canadian-born Geechee-Jamaican writer and filmmaker, raised in Wales and based in London. She is an editor at *bath magg*. Her writing has appeared in *The Oxonian Review*, *Poetry Wales* and the *Guardian*, among others. Her short film *Last Days of the Girl's Kingdom* was produced in collaboration with DAZED and the ICA, and aired on Channel 4's *Random Acts*. In 2021, she was the winner of *The White Review* Poet's Prize and a recipient of an Eric Gregory Award. Her debut pamphlet *Kaleido* is forthcoming with Bad Betty Press in 2022.

Warda Yassin is a British-born Somali poet and teacher based in Sheffield. She was a winner of the 2018 New Poets Prize, and her winning pamphlet *Tea with Cardamom* (Poetry Business) was published in June 2019.

Belinda Zhawi is a Zimbabwean literary and sound artist based in London, author of *Small Inheritances* (ignitionpress, 2018), and experiments with sound/text performance as MA.MOYO. Her work has been featured on various platforms including *The White Review*, NTS, *Boiler Room* & BBC Radio. She's held residencies with Triangle Asterides, Serpentine Galleries and ICA London. Belinda is the co-founder of literary arts platform BORN::FREE.

Acknowledgements

Thank you to the poets, to the whole Canongate familia, and to Sarah who sees me through everything.

Permission Acknowledgements

‘The Acceptance’, ‘And That’ and ‘For Cousin John’ from *All The Names Given* by Raymond Antrobus (Picador, 2021)

‘No Ascension’, ‘Signet’ and ‘Two Black Boys in Paradise’ from *There is (still) love here* by Dean Atta (Nine Arches Press, 2022)

‘There are moments I forget’, ‘You’re’ and ‘Housewarming’ first published in *She Can Still Sing* by Louisa Adjoa Parker, a pamphlet published by flipped eye.

‘Backwards’ and ‘Midnight in the Foreign Food Aisle’ by Warsan Shire. From *Bless the Daughter Raised by a Voice in Her Head* by Warsan Shire published by Chatto & Windus. Copyright © Warsan Shire 2022. Reprinted by permission of The Random House Group Limited. /Used by permission of Random House, an imprint and division of Penguin Random House LLC. All rights reserved.

‘From: Palette for a Portrait of Little Richard’ by Rommi Smith is part of a longer work. It was originally commissioned as part of *Your Local Arena*, an original ‘film meets literature’ concept developed jointly by Lucy Hannah and Speaking Volumes and funded by Arts Council England. The piece was first presented at Bradford Literature Festival.